A practical guide to fathering, revealing the Father and leaving a legacy.

THINGS FATHERS DO

PAUL MANWARING

FOREWORD BY LEIF HETLAND

DEDICATION

To four men who never met in this life:

Ernest, my grandfather. You probably bought me my first meal in a restaurant, you loved life, and you loved God.

Stuart, Sue's grandfather. It was your words of wisdom that guided my career and now we serve the Europe that you dedicated your life to.

Alan, Sue's father. You were the first man that I heard pray for revival. I have never forgotten those all too few Friday nights.

Douglas, my father. Your love for Germany, for family, for God, and for excellence inspire me still.

Thank you. Your influence will never be forgotten.

ACKNOWLEDGMENTS

In the midst of many other pressures in life and keeping the momentum while I settled back into Europe, Chelsea Slade and Kate Jutsum made this book happen.

Chelsea, your ability to protect my voice is a special gift for which I am forever grateful.

Kate, you are one of the most industrious people I know, yet somehow you find time to help me make sense of notes and recordings.

This book about fathers is made possible by two incredible daughters. There is a future book, Things Sons (and daughters) Do. This book is a great example of that next one.

CONTENTS

The Continued Journey Of Fatherhood

FOREWORD

There is no subject more important to every person on earth than God is love. Love is not just something that God is, it is something that He does. I experienced a baptism of love in the year 2000 that totally transformed my life and has given me the grace to receive, become, and release the Father's love in the darkest places in the world. Becoming love and living fully loved begins by first encountering and receiving that very love. God loves us just the way we are, but He wants us to be like Jesus. Jesus came and demonstrated how good the Father is and how loved we are.

If you desire to encounter Papa God's passionate heart for you, I have some good news! *Things Fathers Do* by Paul Manwaring is a gift that I believe has the potential to transform your life and the world you live in. During the past fifteen years, I've had the honor of developing a close friendship with the author and I've observed him as a natural and spiritual father who beautifully reveals our Heavenly Father to those around him. This is a message that needs to be caught just as much as it is taught. You teach what you know, and you reproduce who you are. In *Things Fathers Do*, there is an impartation available for you to receive an upgrade. In the natural and the spiritual, Paul is making this available to all of us who desire to live love out loud. It is the Father's good pleasure to demonstrate His personal, powerful, and passionate love to each of us. God loves me as much as He loves Jesus and that is what makes me extraordinary in an ordinary world. God's kind of love never fails. In His love we have everything!

Things Fathers Do continues to overwhelm me and I've learned over the years that whatever overwhelms you, shapes you. The more you receive God's outrageous love, the more you become like Him, so that your life, family, and workplace will be saturated with what Love does.

Don't settle for less.

Leif Hetland

President, Global Mission Awareness

Author of *Called To Reign*

INTRODUCTION

Dear Dad:

I am just finishing my third book. Yes, I became an author—among other things. Writing this book has been another journey into my heart, memory, and spirit. Many times when I preach about the heart of our Heavenly Father, I talk about you and the day, thirty-two years after you died, that I lay on my bed and had an imaginary conversation with you. As I came to finish this book, it occurred to me to continue that conversation and share with you the impact you've had on this book—and my life—through this letter.

You'd have thought by now—I'm sixty—that I would have forgotten you or "got over" losing you when I was fifteen years old. I have come to realize that "getting over it" is not a realistic goal for anyone who suffers the loss of a loved one at any time in their life. In fact, I often tell those who are grieving to, instead, work to weave the memory of their loved one into the rest of their daily lives. I guess I am living my message. To be honest, it would be impossible to forget you. I look a bit like you, although I have never grown a beard or mustache past ten days' growth. My two sons love the things you loved and my grandsons are beginning to share those passions as well.

A few years ago I wouldn't have been able to write these words. When I realized that abandoning my sonship was unhealthy, I learned to be comfortable with memories of you and I became determined not to focus on what I didn't have, but to make sure that I lived with a desire to become the very thing I lacked. Of course, I would have loved to celebrate life's major events with you during these past forty-five years, share with you my joys of marriage, having sons and grandsons. Sharing these things with you is an experience I will never know, but I have been blessed to enjoy the journey and even more so now that I am aware I am living out things for which you had such value.

Dad, I wrote this book because there are so many people who have experienced absent fathers or fatherlessness and I hope that our story will help them to become the fathers they want to be, regardless of what they had or didn't have. This book is about things fathers do. My goal is to help people, especially fathers, to know that in their doing—in the living out of their lives—they make a difference. And the more confidently we do the right things, the greater the impact of our lives.

One thing I know is that whether our fathers still remain on this earth or not, their influence should never end. I am amazed by the way that DNA gets passed on: family traits get passed from generation to generation, even if the generations never meet.

I find myself with four things in my life that are so clearly influenced by you. We never spoke about what I would do when I grew up, apart from childhood dreams of sports, astronauts, and train drivers. I never had an adult conversation with you about dreams and skill sets, logical choices, and how to pursue my gifting. Yet somehow, your life influenced mine in these profound ways. The first of these is that you were clearly a strategic thinker. I cannot imagine that you would have been selected for your work with Barnes Wallis and the bouncing bomb or sent to Germany to clean up after the war without a mind for strategy. You probably don't know this, but strategy and strategic thinking is also a trait I carry and one that has influenced my career in more ways than one. The second thing that influenced me is when you interviewed with Mum—just before I was born—to work with troubled young men, a job that you only didn't get because it wasn't suitable for a pregnant woman. I also pursued a career working with troubled young men, prisoners, in fact. The third influence is when you became a manager instead. I eventually became the manager of a prison, again following in your footsteps. The fourth influence is that through all of those years you were a regular preacher. I still have your notebook, by the way. I found it in a metal box along with a gun and some engineering and other equipment. Don't worry, I handed the gun in. I even had one of your sermons published in my first book; it was very good.

Those four pieces of your life have so clearly been a part of mine. I have worked as a manager of a juvenile prison, studied, taught, and practiced strategic planning, and now I travel and preach. You gave me more than you knew.

I will always remember how much food was a part of our family. It still is. Memories of what you loved live on, and time spent around the dinner table was a gift you gave me. I even recently discovered how many German foods you loved. You should know that I never visit Germany or Austria without eating a Vienna Schnitzel. You loved quality, and that trait has also been passed on. The cheese, bacon, and ham we sold in Sunnymead's Stores & Post Office were the best, you made sure of it.

These days I have a football and rugby ball always at the ready in the boot of my car, ready for fifteen minutes with my grandson. It reminds me of you, the way you might stop somewhere like Richmond Park and get the cricket stumps out to play a quick game. In all honesty, I can't remember many things that you said but I do remember the things you did and the impact they had on my life. You taught me not to be embarrassed when shopping for gifts for my wife. I still remember all the times you took me with you when shopping for Mum. You taught me to go to crazy lengths to buy the best gifts for my sons by the way you had things delivered for your sons and nephews, and that was before the days of online shopping.

And of course, the last thing you ever did was buy me an SLR camera. Not a day has gone by since that I haven't valued photography.

Dad, you did things, big and small. The way you ran your grocery store and cared for your customers taught me how to pastor people and to love beautiful and excellent things. You always took an interest in the world around you, you treated all women with great respect, and I could go on. You demonstrated so many things.

Most profoundly of all, you showed me all of this before I was fifteen. Perhaps it will encourage others to know the effect that you had, even though you left this life too soon.

This book was birthed when I was creating a memory with my youngest son, which you would have loved: attending the World Cup in Brazil. I still remember sitting with you and watching England win in 1966. We still haven't done it again—win the World Cup, I mean—but we will. I remember how you loved the singing of "Abide With Me" while watching the FA Cup, and of course I remember the hymn you loved to quote when you made a mistake: "Dear Lord and Father of Mankind, Forgive our foolish ways." And I remember your verse from the JB Phillips translation: "Do not let the world squeeze you into its mold."

I became a Christian the day you died. It was both the best and one of the worst days of my life. The things you did meant more than you knew, that's why I wrote this book.

My prayer is that those who read this book will find hope, redemption, and restoration through the telling of our story. Some have also experienced the premature departure of their father, and others never had a good example of an earthly dad. I pray that people will realize the power they have to live life not regretting the deficiencies, but determined to look past their lack and give of themselves so that others—especially their children—won't experience that same lack. Of course, there are those who have had great life experiences with their dads. For them, I hope they will see how blessed they are, and live determined—as you did—to pass that blessing to the generations to come.

Your son,

Paul

REVEAL THE FATHER

SECTION ONE

1. REVEAL THE FATHER

"You are going to be a father." These words are often said at the very start of the journey of fatherhood. The next nine months are filled with appointments, announcements, and celebrations, a nursery to prepare, and in the midst of all of this activity and excitement, great personal change is also about to take place. A woman becomes a mother, a man becomes a father—no application required, no qualification needed. With the arrival of children comes changes in roles and responsibilities, identity shifts, and a whole new set of emotions and experiences. This almost-universal change carries with it the opportunity to paint a picture of fatherhood: not just a picture of who you want to be as a father, but also the image of the Heavenly Father you hope to imitate.

There are many paths that lead to the opportunity of fatherhood. Some choose marriage, and then eventually have natural children. Others are launched into being fathers and mothers through adoption, fostering, and loss or divorce that results in new marriages and blended families coming together. Many of these situations don't come with a period of preparation and meditation on what it might mean to be a parent. In our culture, there is also an ever-increasing opportunity to become a spiritual parent. The traditional family is certainly not the only venue in which fathers are needed.

Whether you are a first-time parent, a spiritual father or mother, or you have been a parent for many years, fatherhood is in equal parts our greatest opportunity and our greatest challenge. The opportunity it presents us, both as fathers and mothers, is that of revealing to the world the greatest father of all: our Father in heaven.

> "So I kneel humbly in awe before the Father of our Lord Jesus, the Messiah, the perfect Father of every father and child in heaven and on the earth." (Ephesians 3:14-15 TPT)

It is this perfect Father who we are privileged to share with the world. We reveal the Father in the things that we say and in the way that we do things—a process which actually begins at birth. At the first sight of a newborn baby, we usually comment on how much he or she looks like the mother or father. As a society, we are not at all surprised by the way offspring—ourselves included—carry similar physical attributes to their fathers and mothers, siblings, or even grandparents. Habits, passions, and behaviors can also be passed on—sometimes without the generations ever meeting—a truth that is celebrated as the way things should be. My two sons are a wonderful example. Neither of them met their paternal or maternal grandfathers, and yet both of them reveal characteristics of these two men. Their love for music, photography, sport, and good food and coffee is evidence of this generational tie. I wish they could have met. My eldest son, in particular, has taken his grandfather's love and talent for music to another level, one of the greatest encouragements of my life.

We grow up aware that we remind people of our ancestors. Now, imagine the spiritual equivalent. We were designed at creation in the image of God and commissioned just after to reproduce; to go forth and multiply. We were made to reproduce a design that does not merely multiply in a random way but actually replicates through DNA. We not only take on the character, habits, and looks of our parents but also of the Father, Son, and Holy Spirit in whose image we were created.

What if, from the moment of our birth, people leaned over our crib and began the comments, "Look at the way he smiles, that's just like the Father"? What if, as we grew up, everyone who met us saw and declared that we display the Father's nature, power, and attributes (Romans 1:20)? If people were constantly reminding us of the similarity between us and our Heavenly Father, imagine what effect that would have on our lives. We may actually believe it ourselves.

It should, therefore, be no surprise that our assignment is to reveal the Father. Genesis 1:26 reads, "Let Us make man in Our image" (NKJV). Our assignment was set at creation: growing up to manifest the looks, behavior, and attributes of the Father. We were made in His image and assigned to reproduce that image. We should embrace this from birth, aspiring to this task before we have endured negative advice and examples from which we will need to recover.

On first hearing it, the assignment to reveal the Father might seem too lofty a goal. We are not God, but we are to be God-like, not in ruling over people, but in being imitators of Him (Galatians 5:1). An historically false perception that God is controlling contributes to a resistance to our assignment, as well as a fear of being prideful and arrogant. I remember the first time I stood with a microphone and said that our assignment, like Christ's, is to declare that, "If you have seen me, then you have seen the Father" (John 14:9). Is it legal? I could hear myself asking. And it is, because the truth in scripture is there for all to see.

My friend Leif Hetland shares this profound truth: when Adam was created, the first face he saw was the Father, the first breath he felt was the Father's, and the first voice he heard was his Father's. As the human race began, so it was meant to continue. Yet, we are more familiar with the physical than we are the spiritual counterpart. The first Adam lost the intimacy of that first contact with the Father, and we have continued to stray from it. The second Adam, Jesus, made that relationship possible again. All of us, through Jesus, are given the privilege of being born again, and that leads us to our great assignment. Being born again enables us to see the face of the Father, hear the voice of the Father, and feel the breath of the Father, so that we can reveal who the Father is.

Several years ago, my son called me from England during his summer holiday. He was very excited because he had been involved in some deliverance ministry and had led a praise party which turned into an opportunity to spiritually re-dig the wells of revival of an historic denomination. The story was immensely encouraging, but it was what he said at the end which changed me. As he finished telling me about his experience, he said, "When I did that, I felt like you, Dad." My son did something he was proud of and he felt like me. It must be every dad's dream to hear those words. I realized that day that we have a Heavenly Father who is also waiting for His kids to say those very words. "When I laid hands on the sick (saw breakthrough, fed the poor), I felt like you, Dad."

When it comes to things fathers do, everything we do has the potential to model the essential role of the Father in another's life. The responsibility for that starts with our natural children as we become the tutor who will imprint fatherhood on the soft clay of a child's life and psyche. As fathers, we are constantly tutoring our children in the ways a father looks and behaves. The power of this role is very real. The question is, will we use that power well or not? We are to model the Heavenly Father to our children so that when they see us, they also see Him.

The more that our experiences reveal the Father to us, the more we will be able to reveal the Father to those around us.

The healthier our experience of fatherhood, the healthier we become. This is the sequence in which we are all divinely involved:

- We are made in the image of God

- We are restored in relationship with Him

- We are called to imitate Jesus

- By imitating Jesus we fulfil our assignment to reveal the Father

- We have everything we need through the Holy Spirit

If you have seen me, you have seen the Father (Paraphrase, John 14:9). This statement either reveals incredible arrogance or unfathomable humility. I would suggest the latter. If we do not embrace this statement, then we will be denying our God-given assignment and the created image given to mankind. Because it is impossible for us to achieve this in our own strength, it requires great humility.

Interestingly, this assignment does not require perfection. If my heart is right and I fail in some way, then I will reveal the Father, not by my failure, but by my heart. If my heart is wrong then whatever I achieve will be undone by my heart attitude. In fact, if I ever think that I have arrived at the perfect representation of the Father, that in itself would undo any accomplishment of revealing God's heart. If my heart is that I must succeed, then my successes will not reveal the Father, they will reveal me. If my heart's desire is to reveal the Father, then no matter what I do I will reveal Him.

This truth is seen in the incredible story of David, the man after God's own heart. He had a catastrophic failure and is still described as the one with the heart like God's. What an incredible encouragement this should be to us all. David, in one of the most significant failures of humanity, became one of the most significant examples of God-likeness.

We have been given the greatest assignment in heaven and on earth: to follow in the footsteps of the One who made it possible for us to have a relationship with the Father. Jesus said that He only did the things He saw the Father doing. Action is clearly a vital aspect of the Christlike and Father-revealing walk of the Christian. In fact, we are molded by the things that are done to us and around us. As we learn to be better fathers and mothers, and as we learn to reveal the Father to the world, an impression will be made on those who receive from us. That impression will determine how those we impact behave as sons and daughters, how they become fathers and mothers, and how they relate to and reveal their Heavenly Father. We may not always get it right, but our assignment is clear. The generations are waiting for us to reveal the Father.

ACTIVATION QUESTIONS

1. In what ways do you think you reveal the Father in your life, work, and relationships? How are you revealing the Father to the world?

2. Spend some time asking the Father how He reveals Himself through you. How can you lean in to what He is doing in and through you?

2. AN INVITATION TO WOMEN

Our culture carries distinct tensions around the roles of men and women, mothers and fathers, which came up again in putting a title to this book. There are things fathers do, but mothers do them, too! Mothers do things that reveal the Father. They often raise children alone and do a great job. Women tend to be better nurturers and homemakers—men are unable to conceive, carry, and nurse children. Women should be represented in every sphere, including in leadership. Like men, women can make great leaders and can also make poor leaders. The challenge for me, whenever the subject of men and women comes up, is to do what I can to correct major imbalances in the way genders have been stereotyped, while not diluting the unique identity of each gender.

One of the ways society has attempted to address the male-female imbalance is through feminism. In the context of the church, women have often been withheld and treated badly under the influence of a religious spirit. That imbalance needs to be addressed. Feminism, I would suggest, fights for equality, but in the church, it often does so by wielding the political spirit against the religious spirit.

In contrast, heaven's way is to give women a place, just as Jesus did throughout His time on earth. In the kingdom, women have a unique place and role, made in the image of God. This does not mean, however, that women are the same as men. It is important that women feel of equal value to men, while not being treated the same way or being expected to parent or lead the same way.

Alongside all the good it has done, the equality movement has also created a false need for women to behave like men, especially in the workplace. When we put this expectation on women, we rob the world of those attributes that women bring when they lead as themselves, out of their unique and equally valuable worldview. We must not allow the pursuit of equality to negate the unique contributions of gender.

Does the title, *Things Fathers Do*, exclude women in any way? I hope that the following clarification will help. I believe that women carry the attributes which I talk about in this book. I believe that God intended that there be a man and a woman, a mother and father, in each family. I believe that we are made in the image of God, male and female. And I believe that men and women are different. A woman can father and a man can mother. They won't do it in the same way, but that doesn't make their contributions any less valuable. Yet, at the same time, there are roles that only a father can perform and roles that only a mother can perform. This is the beauty and the mystery of creation.

While I don't believe in total equality (men cannot carry babies), I do believe in equal value. In the same way, while God has certain qualities that would be more typically associated with women (He is a nurturer and a comforter), I do not think that we need to change His title to "Mother God," or something gender-neutral, in order to reflect that truth.

As a preacher, I work hard to be inclusive with my language, to demonstrate with my words that I draw no distinction between the value of men and women in life and ministry. I do this while also attempting not to dilute the message for the sake of being inclusive. And so I find myself in a place that is not uncommon for me, and that is a place of tension.

Tension always comes with the temptation to try to change something in order to remove discomfort. Tension will often attract the religious or political spirit to remove the tension. But tension itself gives access to energy, and energy creates movement, which is essential for life. So instead of removing tension or discomfort, I would rather keep it alive, knowing that it will give me access to energy. That energy allows me to recognize God in the people around me—male and female—and so become more like Him myself.

I have titled this book *Things Fathers Do*, but it is really things that Father God does and how we can best manifest Him through our lives to the people we love and serve. So don't believe the lie that only men can father, and don't allow gender to disqualify you from revealing the Father. Find the best you that you can, and express it—not in competition or comparison, but in order to reveal the Father, Son, and Holy Spirit. You were made in the image of God, and your assignment is to reveal Him, in your unique way, in every role and relationship throughout your life.

ACTIVATION QUESTIONS

1.   How do you see yourself in the role of being a mother, daughter, wife, or leader? To what extent has today's culture shaped expectations of you in that role, and your expectations of yourself?

2.   What does God want to tell you about your identity in this area, and about how you represent Him to others?

3. HOLY JEALOUSY

"For the Lord, whose name is Jealous, is a jealous God" (Exodus 34:14). For most of us, this is a surprising statement. When we hear the word, "jealousy," it's almost impossible for our minds to create a positive connotation. However, there is a complete difference between being jealous of something or someone and being jealous for something. One will drain you and may even destroy you, and the other will nourish you and draw you toward the source of life.

Jealousy is a gift from God to man that was perverted by the devil before creation. Satan twisted jealousy to draw mankind to himself and themselves, rather than to God and everything that God has for us. Jealousy is an aspect of God that He gave to us in His original design—a part of being made in His image that would allow us to aspire to something greater, to be jealous for life, fullness, and more of God.

"For I, the Lord your God, am a jealous God" (Exodus 20:5). God is jealous for us to have what is ours, the things put in us at creation as He made us in His image. That is the nature of His jealousy. God has no need to be jealous of something, there is nothing better or greater for Him to have. Rather, He is jealous for us to have access to everything that is ours. He is jealous for us to know Him, to be close to Him because He knows that there is nothing better for us.

Jealousy, as we have always known it, is one of the most destructive forces on planet earth, driving men to greater and greater sin as we continually miss the mark of God's truth and love. Our jealousy of people and things removes us farther from God. Yet jealousy for God draws us to Him and invites us to be like Him. He is jealous for us to be like Him and with Him, because He knows that to be like Him is nourishment for us, and that the closer we are to Him the more we become fully alive.

Healthy, holy jealousy will raise the bar on the potential of our lives. Surely, the ultimate God-likeness is to be a good father. Our good Father is a jealous God, not jealous of anyone or anything else in the entire universe, but jealous for us. As His creation and His imitators (Ephesians 5:1), it is only right that we become jealous for being more like Him—jealous for our children, families, and communities to have access to everything which is theirs. To be jealous for the greatest role which man has been given is a worthy quest. Therefore, to understand its evil twin and overcome it will set us on course for the rest of our journey.

Much of the energy for this book arose out of a trip I took with my youngest son during the summer of 2014. We traveled to Brazil where we were able to fulfill a dream of seeing our national team, England, play in the World Cup. It was truly the trip of a lifetime. We agreed on the trip that it is reasonable to conclude that while England invented the game of football (soccer), the Brazilians have perfected it. However, the clinical and beautiful win by the German national team demonstrated that perfecting the game is not exclusive to Brazil.

When I returned, I used some of my experiences in a sermon on the subject of things fathers do. As I was preparing my message, I was aware that hearing about such a trip might be difficult for some who perhaps don't have the means or capability of fulfilling such a dream with their sons or daughters.

The last thing I wanted to do was create reasons for jealousy or envy. I also try not to take the privilege of my position for granted, as I am extremely blessed in getting to travel the world.

At that moment, I realized that I wanted to create a different kind of jealousy, not of something but for something. It is a very important distinction: one leads to sin, the other leads to a greater awareness of our potential. Fathers should create jealousy for things. The purpose of this book is to create in each of you jealousy for these attributes, actions, and outcomes. The stories I tell and the examples I give are not to make you jealous of the experiences I've had, but to make you jealous for the outcome: a revelation and restoration of our roles as sons and fathers. Not all of you will want to watch World Cup soccer with your sons, but all of you would want the relational experience and outcome which such a moment can produce.

Being jealous *of* something leads to feeling sorry for oneself, a reflection on what you don't have and the myriad flawed reasons why you don't have it. It will lead to perverted plans to get the things you are jealous of and fail to allow you to pursue the things for which you are rightly jealous. Jealousy *for* something creates desire, it actually opens up your soul to questions that are creative and outward-focused instead of negative and self-pitying.

Jealousy which arises from perverted desires is listed alongside many other sins in Galatians 5:19-21. Perversion is a different version of what was originally intended. That is exactly what the devil does to us; he gives us another version of something for which we were created. The jealousy we have known is another version, a false version, which will lead us away from God instead of to Him, away from our destiny instead of towards it. False jealousy will pay a price. It costs us the price of our souls as we attempt to have more than our neighbors and are willing to do anything to get it. "For what will it profit a man if he gains the whole world, and loses his own soul?" (Mark 8:36). God's jealousy was willing to pay the ultimate price: sending His son so that we could be more like Him and have full access to Him.

This is not the only aspect of the kingdom that was twisted away from its original purpose. Jealousy sits alongside shame and fear as gifts from God that have been perverted by the fall of satan and man. Not only have they become three weapons that can drag us down and away from our calling and potential, but they prevent us from accessing the strength for which they were originally given. They were meant as gifts from God given for our safety.

Jealousy was given to us to make us desire all things good and God-like. Shame, on the other hand, was given to us to keep us in the presence of God. It enables us to anticipate the effect or outcome of our actions. Fear was given to us for our protection from harm. The fear of the Lord is an awareness of the harm which comes if we do not stay in right relationship with Him.

Jesus paid the ultimate price for us to live like this. Many of us have been raised in churches that created an impression that righteousness was a set of rules and that justice was what happened when we broke the rules. Righteousness is an invitation to be like God, to be in right standing with Him, and justice is the provision by Jesus of everything we need to accept the invitation. Once we realize this and accept the invitation, then our journey can truly and fully begin as we step into the greatest assignment that there has ever been: revealing the Father.

Jesus' death and resurrection make possible our ability to jealously long to be like Him and His Father. One of the most astonishing verses I have ever read is when Jesus tells us that we will do greater works than even He did (John 14:12). This is extraordinary, unbelievable in so many respects, and yet because of our journey of faith, believable. It is Christ's aspiration for us, and therefore should be our aspiration for ourselves.

This is holy jealousy that we must steward; jealousy that causes tension as we learn to walk in boldness and confidence, with humility. This is our assignment: to go into all the world and to perform the works of Jesus. We must aspire to do more than He did, requiring boldness and confidence in the anointing and gifts we carry, all the while not allowing ourselves to step into pride or arrogance, both of which will lead us back to false jealousy.

Stewarding this tension is key to our journey of revealing the Father and doing the things fathers do. This is how I seek to live, not because I have achieved or attained all I need, but because I am jealous for the attributes of the Father. This gift of jealousy, kept pure, will lead us further on our journey of becoming like our good and perfect Father.

ACTIVATION QUESTIONS
1. Take a few minutes to look over your life with Jesus. Where do you see healthy, holy jealousy, and where is there false jealousy? Ask Jesus what you need to do to deal with the areas of false jealousy.

2.   Have you avoided being jealous for things because of the negative side of unhealthy jealousy? What areas do you need to reach forward in and be jealous for?

4. EVERYONE NEEDS ADOPTING

In my first book, *What on Earth is Glory*, I describe some of my journey. Nineteen years of my adult life was spent working in prisons, an environment that is known for a clientele lacking positive experiences of sonship and fatherhood. My experience with the broken and fatherless is a major contributor to my passion for teaching on the priority of sonship. I saw those who had never received love look for love in all the wrong places. I saw men whose inner lives were so frustrated that anger and violence became their norm.

When I was working in one particular prison in the late 1980s, I had regular, although impromptu, meetings with the prison's art teacher. She would often drop into my office on her way to lunch and talk about any number of subjects. She was extremely creative and we first connected over a discussion about the amazing art produced by prisoners. Art and creativity have always been an interest of mine and I never cease to marvel at the art created in even the darkest of places. John Bunyan, for example, began writing the classic Christian allegory, *Pilgrim's Progress*, while he was in prison. My conversations with the art teacher, however, didn't stop at art. We covered much ground, from education to personal faith and family life.

The environment of prison can sometimes be a very stimulating one, despite the overwhelming presence of so many negative life experiences all in one place. The unique environment often causes those working within a prison to think and discuss issues which may not be commonly thought about or shared. In this case, it caused us to ask questions about ourselves as we observed the lives of those incarcerated. We discussed how so many of the men in prison had not had the same chances in life as we had. These conversations were the kind that would remind us of why we worked there. They also reminded us of the grace in our lives.

One day the conversation between the art teacher and I became much more personal. She was not only an artist but a very well educated woman who had been adopted by a Jewish family. In the midst of our conversation, I made a comment that being born was one thing, but being adopted was the highest standard of family. I explained that it is the highest standard of being chosen and loved and made to feel part of a family. She had never thought of her life this way, instead, looking at what she had lacked rather than what she had been given. I don't remember how the conversation began that day, but I do know how it ended. My art teacher friend began crying tears of joy, gratitude, and revelation. In my office that day, she saw that her adoption, even to a family with a specific faith which she had not fully embraced, was a great privilege and a powerful statement about her value as a daughter.

Raising sons and daughters must always include the dimension of adoption: wanting, embracing, and fully incorporating others into our family, starting of course with our own children. This understanding was reinforced again more recently as I heard a woman talk about her three adopted children. She said that from the first day the children came into her home, she and her husband told them that they were not living "Plan B" for their lives. Through this statement, she is showing her adopted children that they are fully accepted into the family.

The truth is that we all need to be adopted. This is shown through the life of Jesus. He was raised in the house of His adopted father, Joseph. At His baptism, He was once again adopted through the Father's declaration, "This is My beloved son, in whom I am well pleased" (Matthew 3:17). If Jesus needed this, then we most certainly do as well. A son or daughter grows to their fullest potential when they arrive at a point of knowing that they belong, not just because they were born, but because they are a member of the family, a bearer of the family name.

Isaiah 9:6 declares, "To us a child is born, to us a son is given." A child is an offspring, but a son is a bearer of the family name. The prophecy in Isaiah 9 is about Jesus, the one who would be called, "Wonderful Counselor, Mighty God, Eternal Father, Prince of Peace." Isaiah later prophesied that these titles and the entire government would not be placed on the shoulders of a child, but a son. Before Jesus' public ministry began, He was publicly baptized and affirmed by the Father. Heaven's entire family was present, heaven and earth were connected and the transition from earth's offspring to Son of man and Son of God was manifest as the government of heaven was placed on the shoulders of the Son.

Everyone is born a child and all of us are given the opportunity to be born again as sons and daughters. The journey is designed to take us from birth to adoption. This is where our lives truly begin. Like Jesus, we are to receive baptism, be affirmed by the Father, filled by the Holy Spirit, and made ready for our assignment as the adopted sons and daughters of the King. The scene at Jesus' baptism is played out every time one of us is born again through the blood of Jesus, affirmed by the Father, and filled with the Holy Spirit. The Father, Son, and

Holy Spirit are present and we are adopted into heaven's royal family.

The beauty and truth of adoption are illustrated through the daughter-in-law. A woman falls in love with a son, takes the family name (in many cultures), and becomes a joint heir with her husband. This beautifully parallels our relationship with Christ. We are able to experience such a journey and relationship because of a love which is born out of His love for us. It is His love for us which gives us the capacity to love in the first place. In fact, Jesus declared that we would be known as Christians because of our love. It is the very thing that inspires us to take on the family name. We are forever known as followers of Jesus. Lastly, we become joint heirs, an unbelievable privilege as we become partakers in the inheritance for which He gave His life (Romans 8:17). In this respect, we will be daughters-in-law for all eternity: we fall in love, take the family name, and become joint heirs with the Son.

And so we are adopted as sons and daughters. We follow in the footsteps of Jesus, the son who had no natural earthly father and the father who had no natural earthly sons. Before we further explore the things fathers do, we must start here. If we do not understand the value and importance of our own adoption journey, then everything we do for the King and His kingdom will become a set of tasks or responsibilities, instead of the expression of an adopted and much-loved member of the family. Valuing our own adoption into the kingdom is an essential step towards becoming a father and will empower who we are and all that we do. It is the intimacy of this adoption that we will continue to learn all the days of our lives, and into eternity.

ACTIVATION QUESTIONS

1. To what degree have you embraced your adoption into heaven's royal family? What difference has this made in your own walk?

2. In this chapter, we learn that we are to "Receive baptism, be affirmed by the Father, and filled by the Holy Spirit." Where are you on this journey?

5. THE JOURNEY OF SONSHIP

My father died when I was fifteen years of age, an event which made me fatherless in the natural far too early. My experience is not an uncommon one, as fatherlessness is a pervasive characteristic of our world. There are many who never knew their father, were abandoned, or were even abused and hurt by their father or father figures in their lives. I have come to believe that fatherlessness is perhaps the single greatest problem on earth and is the very curse of Malachi 4:6: "And he shall turn the heart of the fathers to the children, and the heart of the children to their fathers, lest I come and smite the earth with a curse" (KJV).

Our fathers and mothers are instruments to show us how to relate to other people as well as how to relate to our Heavenly Father and His triune family. Lacking the human tutor to show how the Heavenly Father relates to us is a deficit for Christian and non-Christian alike. The impact of fatherlessness can range from creating driven people who perform for attention or to avoid punishment, to those with no boundaries, who find themselves in lives of extremes: from self-hatred to crime, jail or social dysfunction, and a myriad of other expressions.

The idea of a curse is often thought to be highly spiritual, but I would suggest that more often than not a curse begins in the natural. For example, let's compare curses to blessings. It is a blessing to be raised in a Christian family, with generations of parents who have provided a practical experience of love, faithfulness, and Christian principles for their children. The result is a blessing that is both natural and spiritual. The same applies to curses. They, too, can start in the practical and, from generation to generation, influence an individual's experience of this world, pushing them further away from a relationship with God.

During my first twenty-five years as a believer, I was not exposed to a great deal of any teaching on inner healing, the Father heart of God, or sonship. I regarded myself as having a good grasp of relationships, when in reality I was lacking in numerous human experiences:

- My father died when I was fifteen.

- My wife's father died one year after I met her.

- I have a sister and no brothers.

- I have sons and no daughters.

- None of the immediate women in my life have had a father or father-in-law present for much, or any, of their adult lives.

- I worked in male prisons for nineteen years.

Then one day, a simple revelation caused me to begin to grow in my awareness of the relational emphasis of heaven. I had just been asked to build a new organization and so as I sat listening to a favorite teacher, I asked God a question: How do you father an organization? The answer came to me rather quickly: In order to father an organization, you have to first be a son.

Fathering an organization was not a new experience for me. As the Senior Manager of a prison, I was a father to many prisoners and staff alike. But perhaps I had been missing an element of fatherhood in my tenure as a prison manager. As I sat contemplating this, I heard God's voice again speak to my heart about sonship. This time, however, His words cut into my heart. He revealed to me that I stopped being a son the day my father died.

I began to see that my relational deficits were real and that I had much to learn. Every healthy relational dynamic on earth has the potential to tutor us in how the heavenly family relates to each other and to us, and therefore how we can relate to them. Likewise, every unhealthy relationship can distort our ability to relate to the Trinity and every deficit leaves us with gaps in our experience. Yet, deficits are an invitation for God to redeem.

After my father died, I remember the well-meaning words of so many individuals as they slapped me on the back and told me that I was the man of the house now. There was truth in it; my father's death left my mother, sister, and me with a house and a small business. There was much to be done and I was a competent and hard-working young man. Like far too many people on this earth, adulthood was thrust upon me before I had the chance to fully embrace the experiences of childhood.

I did many things right over the years which would be considered father-like, however, my actions came from head knowledge, or a feeling of responsibility, rather than from the heart. God's words to me carried with them a revelatory sting as I finally understood that I had bypassed the rite of passage from child to son to father. I went from child to adult, and responsibility and duty became my guide. Competence and learning can teach us all many things, but if they bypass the heart, then they will almost certainly need to be revisited later in life. The truth of becoming "the man of the house" actually created a lie in my life.

My immediate response to God's revelation was to repent. The best definition of repentance is to change the way you think. Even this definition has been largely associated with repentance from sin, which is only half of the truth contained in Romans 3:23: "All have sinned and fallen short of the Glory." Repentance from sin is necessary, but it is repentance unto the greater truth which is an essential ingredient. This repentance act alone requires a degree of revelation. We are so accustomed to repenting of things which we have done or failed to do, that to repent of something which we had no control over does not come naturally to us. And so I repented unto sonship, a prayer which began a lifelong journey.

My next step on this journey was to deal with my feelings toward what I now saw as wasted years. Joel 2:25 was immediately in my mind: "And I will restore to you the years that the locust hath eaten" (KJV). *How can thirty-two years of fatherlessness be restored?* I thought. Those years were gone, but what I didn't realize was that the value that had been absent from those years could be restored into the present day.

At that time, I was reading *The Supernatural Power of a Transformed Mind,* by Bill Johnson. I don't exactly know how I made the connection, but I correlated a chapter on the sanctified imagination with my predicament of fatherlessness. I realized that I had thirty-two years without any awareness of a father's voice in my head. I had certainly been around men and fathers, but I can only conclude that in my efforts to be a responsible man and father, none of their voices had impacted the deeply hidden son inside of me. It wasn't their fault, it was mine. Since I had been relatively "successful" in life I had avoided the kind of crash which might necessitate an intervention and reveal my dysfunction in that area.

On reading about sanctified imagination, I did something which can easily be misinterpreted. I lay on my bed and, in my imagination, I had a conversation with my dad. It was, in all respects, a conversation within my imagination, not a conversation with the spirit of a dead man. However, it was one of the most powerful things I have done and it changed me. I simply imagined myself telling him about my life. I described my wife and my sons, my career, my successes and failures, the days I wish that he had been there, and the days which I am glad that he wasn't. At the end of the conversation, I knew that I was changed. My imagination enabled forgotten voices of encouragement and affirmation from my father to be awoken.

From that moment, my thinking was completely restored. My mind began to access the things I had been told or heard or experienced, of which adulthood had denied or obscured the value. I began to experience life from the perspective of a son, rather than that of an orphan. Since then, I have been aware in my imagination of someone cheering me on from the great cloud (or crowd) of witnesses. The illustrations and changes since then are endless, as are the ways in which my Heavenly Father has continued to restore the years and give me relational opportunities which I never dreamed I would have.

Much has been written about the spirit of adoption and journeys from orphan to son, and each revelation helps us to relate better on earth and to experience our Father in heaven. From my own experience, I highly recommend the two steps which I took on my journey. They changed me and they can change you. Whatever the life circumstance that has resulted in fatherlessness, or caused you to stop being a son or daughter, start with repentance and follow it with a conversation in your imagination with your father. If a conversation with your earthly father is too painful, have the same conversation with God; He too wants to hear your life story.

I believe your restoration, like mine, can be immediate. Restoration suggests to me a beautiful play on words: there are things in the store again. Within days of my encounter with God and my conversation with my dad, a spiritual father of mine gave me a gift. It was the first time in thirty-two years that I remember a father giving me something unsought and unexpected. This person was not aware of the things God was doing in my heart regarding sonship and fatherhood. He simply came to me as a father with a gift, and I was able to receive it as a son.

If you have experienced fatherlessness or have in any way hardened your heart to being a son or a daughter, repent, not just from sin but unto the glory of sonship and daughtership. Everyone needs to be adopted into the kingdom, and we all have an opportunity to learn and understand what it is to be a child of the King and a father or mother to the nations. Let this prayer become your own, because this is the journey of sonship, and it lasts a lifetime.

Father, today I change the way I think and turn towards being a son (or daughter). I forgive myself for being driven to find love and acceptance and I choose the full acceptance of being Your son, not just in turning from sinful behavior as I have done in the past, but choosing You as Father and embracing my identity as a son. Forgive me for being driven, for thinking that I can perform for love or work hard to avoid punishment. Today I choose to know that I am loved and that my true identity is as Your son.

ACTIVATION QUESTIONS

1. Ask God to show you any point at which you stopped being a son or a daughter. If you identify one, start with repentance and follow it with a conversation in your imagination with your father, or your Heavenly Father.

2. Ask God what He has in store for you in the future as His son or daughter.

6. OVERCOMING LIES: PART ONE

At some point in their lives, the majority of men aspire to become fathers. When they do, their experience ranges from feeling excited to feeling completely unqualified or even intimidated. Others may become fathers before they ever have a chance to aspire to or plan for the role. The journey to being a father evokes many emotions, fears, anxieties, and triggers. I doubt that there are many titles in life that awaken as many emotions.

For some, fatherhood elicits associations with the positive experiences of fathers from childhood. For others, it is the opposite: in place of excitement and pride is fear and doubt. Fatherhood reveals a litany of disqualifying obstacles in our lives. These obstacles, however, create in us the awareness of what we lack or what we believe we lack. When we are aware of our deficiencies, it motivates us to pursue that very thing we are lacking; it motivates us toward breakthrough.

Being a father doesn't require any formal qualifications. Rather, it is something that God planned for us to be prepared and trained for through the environment and experience of family. Wherever you are on the fatherhood spectrum—experiencing aspiration, desire, or a sense of inadequacy—a willingness to do the very thing for which you are unqualified may be the critical factor that leads to your qualification. However severe our deficits, God is willing and available to help us in our weakness. He qualifies those who are unqualified.

Have you ever noticed that behind the lives of many who share great revelation and insight is pain or dramatic encounter with God and truth? I often think of the genius of God that He would take a man who dramatically and radically persecuted the church, and allow him to become the primary apostle of the New Testament. If ever there was a man disqualified it would be the Apostle Paul. Yet, through an encounter with God, he became one of the greatest Christian leaders and founders. How many times did he fight a mental battle of feeling disqualified by his previous behavior and alliances? Did he feel inadequate leading alongside apostles who had actually walked with Jesus?

There are moments, choices, and experiences in your life that seek to disqualify you. These things, whatever they may be, can become your focus, drawing you away from the breakthrough and victory available to you and to others. Do not allow those things to achieve their goal of disqualifying you. Instead, allow your obstacles to work to your advantage. You will be amazed as you join the ranks of those whose deficits have pushed them to become the greatest champions.

Overcoming our deficits is a rich and rewarding experience. While I am the very proud father of two sons and two grandsons, I often quip that I "specialize" in boys. When it comes to my spiritual children, however, I tend to specialize in daughters. Out of my deficit (not that I have one regret about only having sons), I pursued opportunities to learn to father daughters. My deficit could have disqualified me, but I believe it has instead become the very thing that qualified me. While in the natural I am a father to only sons, I have had the privilege of walking a spiritual daughter down the aisle, an unforgettable moment in my life.

An entire book could be written on the things we need to overcome on the way to becoming a father. There are mindsets, the lies that prevent us from fully manifesting a father's heart. Life can so easily be steered by what we don't have, or by the negative things we are led to believe. Fatherhood attracts these lies and obstacles. The physical and emotional journey to becoming a father is very real, but the continuing journey of being a father is equally real. It is necessary to deal with the obstacles, the deficits, and the lies on our way to being fathers, and it will be a part of our journey for the remainder of our lives. Becoming a father is an invitation to a lifetime of overcoming.

The central person of our faith is a son who did not have a natural, earthly father. He will be forever known as Eternal Father even though He had no earthly children. In fact, He will also be known as the son of David. That means for all eternity He will be known as the son of an imperfect father. That should encourage all of us that the quality of the father does not determine the quality of the son. It is my hope that this reality creates in us a desire to grow as sons and daughters and mothers and fathers, regardless of our earthly experiences, our deficits, or the lies we have believed.

What are the lies and obstacles that you have the opportunity to overcome? The goal of a lie is to keep us from the truth, but it doesn't stop there. The lies we believe are very often related to our specific destiny and calling. They masquerade as truth and become the foundation for the way we think and behave. We do not recognize them as lies until they are revealed for what they are. When we recognize a lie for what it is, it becomes the foundation for greater revelation. It becomes an obstacle we get to overcome.

This was the very experience of the younger son in the parable in Luke 15. After abandoning his family and squandering his inheritance, he eventually came to his right mind or—as I consider it—he realized what he was not. He realized he wasn't a son and no longer had a father in his life. He came face to face with not only his lack but the lies that led him there. If we can see that the lies and obstacles we face are related to our destiny, then we will develop the courage and the motivation to overcome them and—like the younger brother in Luke 15—turn our hearts and ourselves toward the Father.

There are three stages to identifying and overcoming lies in your life. While it doesn't always feel simple in the process, revealing a lie really is simple. First, ask yourself if you agree that this obstacle you are facing is, in fact, a lie. Secondly, ask the Father if it is, in fact, a lie. And thirdly, ask yourself how to replace the lie with the truth.

I encourage you to take these three steps into consideration as we continue our journey of overcoming lies in the following chapter. Take some time to consider your deficits and how they have encouraged you toward breakthrough. If you have never looked at lack in that way, then take some time to imagine how the things you lack might be the door to the very breakthrough you have been seeking. And as you do, prepare yourself to overcome your lies, deficits, and obstacles.

ACTIVATION QUESTIONS

1. How do you feel when you consider being or becoming a father, be it natural or spiritual?

2. Ask God if there is a lie you are believing about yourself as a father, or about Him. What truth does He want to give you to replace that lie?

7. OVERCOMING LIES: PART TWO

We are all called to be fathers and mothers both in natural relationships, with our own offspring, and spiritually for those around us in need of parenting. It is important to deal with anything in our thinking that undermines our qualification for this great assignment. The good news is, dealing with the lies that hinder us may not be as difficult as you might think.

This chapter will outline five lies that prevent us from accepting or embracing fatherhood. While this is not a comprehensive list, I believe these lies are some of the most common that we face as human beings.

1. **I can't father people unless I am "better" than them in their gift or calling.**
    I want to start with this obstacle because the revelation of this lie recently took me by surprise. By the time we get to the end of this section, we should all be laughing at this lie, just as my friend and colleague Steve Backlund teaches in his book, *Let's Just Laugh At That*. It may take a personal journey before we are able to laugh at this lie, but when we do, we will see that this giant obstacle is but a tiny pebble.

The revelation I experienced regarding this lie is connected to a prophecy I received in February 2012. One particular aspect of the prophetic word was that I would raise up young evangelists. Honestly, this seemed almost ridiculous to me at the time. How could I possibly father young evangelists when I did not see myself as an evangelist? My head was immediately juggling who I considered myself to be with the prophetic word and a strong desire to maintain my integrity to what I knew to be an assignment from God.

Shortly after I received the prophetic word, I found myself in the company of many young evangelists. I was attracted to their message, to their passion, and their lifestyle. Yet, I knew it was not my role to become like them, nor did my daily life give me the space to explore that lifestyle. Instead, I was experiencing a manifestation of the divine tension caused by the prophetic. A true prophetic word foretells a future scenario, highlighting the difference between what is and what is prophesied to be.

One day, I had the opportunity to pray for an experienced evangelist, Jean Luc Trachsel. It turned out to be a unique moment for both me and him. After I prayed for him, he told me that he received prayer from many evangelists, but that it always felt like a brother praying for him, using the prayer as an opportunity to instruct or comment on technique. He went on to say that when I prayed for him, it felt like he was receiving the prayer and covering of a father. He did not know anything about me or my prophetic journey.

As we stood talking, I remembered the statement Paul made that there are many teachers but not many fathers (1 Corinthians 4:15). Could it be that sometimes brothers can feel like teachers? I am not a fellow evangelist (a brother)—my past does not qualify me in that role—but I am assigned to father evangelists. That day my thinking changed. I am not called to teach evangelists or even do what they are called to do. In other words, I am not required to be greater at evangelism in order to be a father to evangelists.

In fact, this lie that we must be better than those we are fathering makes no sense if we apply it to other areas of life, most notably the natural father-son relationship. I have two sons, one of whom is a very accomplished musician. I, on the other hand, can list my musical accomplishments as the ability to play a CD or an MP3. But I am his father, and I am very capable of encouraging him, cheering him on, and positioning him for success, all without having my own musical abilities. What is more, due to our relationship, I have no doubt that he values my non-musical encouragement as highly as he does the encouragement from experts or other musicians.

By limiting our fathering to those that have similar skills or gifts, we rob others of the encouragement and love that they need. Also, if we only father people in areas of our strength, we will be tempted to link our fathering to instruction rather than to encouraging others out of relationship and honor. People have many instructors, and they may even have many brothers, but they don't have many fathers. The lie that we cannot father apart from our skills and gifts is robbing the world of a father's encouragement, love, and belief.

Fathering is not a matter of the mind, it is a matter of the heart; making our hearts available and connecting with the hearts of sons and daughters in our lives.

2. I can't be a father because I've never had children.

Earthly, physical deficits do not determine our ability as fathers and mothers. My wife, Sue, and I have two natural sons. We love them dearly, they are our pride and joy. Our journey to having our sons included four years of infertility and a miscarriage. When our second son was born as the result of a miraculous healing, we were overjoyed that our first son would have a brother.

As I moved into the world of pastoring and leading people, I became aware that I lacked the experience of fathering daughters. I had no previous use of the word daughter in my daily life. I ran a male prison, had two sons, and none of the females in my immediate family had a living father. In October 2001, however, God gave me the impression that I needed to learn how to father daughters. My initial response was to laugh, but it wasn't long before the impression became an obvious and daily part of my journey.

Fast forward to 2006. Sue and I were flying back to the USA after our eldest son's wedding. The common belief is that the really tough role at a wedding is that of the father of the bride, and since I was not him, I had nothing to be worried about, right? After the wedding, I was feeling very emotional and I asked God why I felt so exhausted, emotional, and wiped out. This simple, yet profound thought came to me: You are emotional because yesterday you got a glimpse into My heart. God is the father of the groom and He is waiting for His son to marry His bride. In what I thought was my deficit, not being the father of the bride, there was an opportunity for me to experience a fresh revelation of fatherhood.

More recently, when my wife and I were visiting a friend who had just given birth to a second child after a gap of thirteen years, I found myself with a unique opportunity and challenge. I was near to one of my favorite cities and had planned a quiet day, wandering with my camera, doing some personal shopping, and enjoying a good cup of coffee in one of the numerous craft coffee shops. However, another option arose and that was to take a thirteen-year-old "daughter" shopping. It would give my wife some time alone with her friend and newborn baby. I knew it would be fun, even if there was some sacrifice involved. As it turned out, it was one of those experiences that I never knew I was missing. When the day was over, I jotted down the things I learned from shopping with a thirteen-year-old daughter.

1. Don't bother taking the camera.

2. If in doubt, buy both.

3. If dressed well, a "father and daughter" will always be sent to the designer section of the store.

Despite being a father of sons, that day I felt like I had succeeded as a father in a new way. We had fun, we laughed, and we bought two purses instead of one, learning that sometimes it is impossible for a daughter to be expected to choose. I didn't get to take as many photos as I would have liked, but I didn't miss out on my coffee and we laughed as much as any father and daughter could possibly have done.

I really don't think that it would ever have occurred to that young lady that I was unqualified for the task of fathering a teenage girl. The lie that the absence of natural children disqualifies you can be easily undone if we take the opportunities we are given to parent. The lie's undoing can look like encouraging and cheering on from the touchline of people's lives, giving what we have to give rather than being paralyzed by the overemphasis of what we lack.

3. I haven't got my own life together yet.

This is the lie we use to postpone our contribution to others, because the truth is, none of us will fully arrive this side of heaven. If we are not careful, our postponement could be lifelong, and potential recipients of our love will never receive what we have to give.

I often laugh (silently, of course) when I hear someone comment that they don't have their act together. The truth is, even when we do get our "act" together, it will sadly still be an act. One of the great needs in the world today is authenticity and vulnerability. People in need of fathers and mothers do not need an act to live up to, or a perfect life to emulate. They need real. They need fathers who know that they don't have it all together but are willing to impart the lessons learned and encourage others on their journey through mistakes, trials, and opportunities.

If the enemy can cause us to focus on our weaknesses and failures, he can keep us paralyzed from action. Once again, the view from our deficit will give substance to what we do and what we have achieved. It will place us in the camp of the life-long learners, learning as we father others and creating venues for shared growth. One of the things I most love about our faith and the Bible is that it contains the warts of all of our forefathers. Apart from Jesus, none of them were perfect and many of them were almost the exact opposite of perfection. Yet, the lessons they taught us stand for eternity. Jesus will be known as the son of David for all eternity, the son of a murdering adulterer. Remember, the quality of a father does not determine the quality of the son. Don't let your deficits stop you from fathering, they don't have to be contagious.

Lies of any kind focus on what isn't true: that is their nature. As fathers, it is our job to release hope and truth. As Francis Frangipane wrote in *Three Battlefields*, "Any area of your life which is not glistening with Hope is under the influence of a lie." Life is not about achievement, but about a heart which leans on faith, hope, and love.

4. I don't have a natural father as a role model.

As a generation, there exists more potential for natural fatherlessness than ever before, caused by reasons as diverse as casual relationships, the same-sex agenda, sperm donors, and other medical developments. However, our generation is also more aware than ever before that there is a spiritual solution that outweighs every deficit. So many fathers and mothers have given us revelation and insights, from Floyd McClung's brilliant *Father Heart of God*, to Jack Frost's *Experiencing the Father's Embrace,* and today's myriad of authors and speakers on the subject. Our greatest obstacle is that we don't merely become familiar with the language of fatherhood and sonship, but that we apply the message and allow our hearts and minds to be on a lifelong journey of transformation to sonship and daughtership.

In many respects, how our fathering deficit occurred isn't as important as the revelation of what we are lacking and the understanding that it does not end there. As I wrote previously, my journey back to sonship began with the revelation that I had stopped being a son. I realized that there was a way back, that this was not just a natural, incurable consequence of loss, absence or abuse, but a state of the heart, and that it could and should be restored in every case, no exceptions. If, for whatever reason, you have stopped being a son or daughter, repentance is the place to start. It is important to realize that repentance is not a one time act, but rather a turning towards God, a realization of a higher calling and a way of life that transcends life as it was prior to repentance. Don't be hard on yourself, if you can keep turning towards God, then you are on track.

I can promise you that this will erase the lie that you can't be a father because of your deficient relationship with your own father. What you thought would disqualify you will actually qualify you for greater things than you ever imagined. Your deficit can become the encouragement you need to press beyond your lack, stepping into a realm you only thought was reserved for others.

5.   I will only disappoint those I am fathering.

Many of us struggle with the lie that we will let people down and therefore, we cannot risk being a father to them. Like many lies, this one actually starts with a truth. The truth is that we will let people down. While this is not intentional, there will come a moment when we do something—or don't do something—that will cause disappointment in the life of a son or daughter. It is an essential part of life's journey of learning. The lie hidden within this truth is that the disappointment we create will disqualify us. It is such a profound lie that it keeps us from becoming fathers. The goal, however, is not to avoid disappointment, but to journey through it. This alone can bring strength and growth to the relationship.

This is especially true when someone has already been let down by a father or father figure. We don't want to add to someone's "father wounds," of course. However, not risking relationship will most certainly add rejection to that individual's life. Overcoming the lie means that we risk relationship despite the fact that there will be disappointments.

Writing this, I am very aware that my view of life is limited by my own experience. Some of you may have other lies which are preventing you from stepping in to the fullness of what God has for you as fathers. Whatever these lies may be, I encourage you to spend some time reflecting. There are so many possible lies, but the truth available to you will astound you. A natural deficit of failure doesn't have to disqualify you. In fact, it will almost certainly qualify you as a father who has lived a real and authentic life, and out of that you will find you have more to give.

ACTIVATION QUESTIONS:

1. Do you personally identify with any of the lies explained in this chapter? Where did those lies come from? Is there anyone you need to forgive?

2. Ask God what truth He wants to replace the lies with. What has He given you in exchange for the areas in which you have felt a deficit?

THINGS
FATHERS
DO

SECTION TWO

8. FATHERS DO THINGS

The very first passages of the Bible reveal incredible truths; yet, behind the grandeur of the creation story is one truth that we have almost all read and overlooked. The first depiction of Creator God is of Him doing something; taking action. On that very first day in time, the Father of all, Creator, God Most High, did something. He created, He made, and He fashioned out of who He is.

Someone, somewhere once said that artists do two things: they copy and they express themselves. God had nothing to copy, so He just expressed Himself. The result of that is all of creation, including us. Just as our Father in Heaven expresses Himself, we who are made in the image of the heavenly, royal family are also created to do things—and none more than fathers.

There is a catchy phrase that gets tossed around claiming that we are human beings rather than human doings. This clever play on words helps me at times to bring some needed recalibration to my life when I allow myself to get too busy. However, it was never meant to be left as a prescription for life. I often get to know people by discovering what they do—for work, for fun, and for rest. These details give me great insight into who someone is, acting as a mirror to reflect back to them who they are, based on the various doings of their lives. Of course, if all that someone has is what they do, then they will find their identity there. If what they do comes from knowing who they are, however, then the result is a life of great strength and purpose.

Life simply cannot be reduced to being or doing alone. You cannot have one without the other. We do not have a passive God and equally, we ourselves should not be passive. As fathers, especially, passivity is not an option, nor do we find that it is natural to us. Jesus, as the son of God, was very clear on this matter when He said, "Did you not know that I must be about my Father's business?" (Luke 2:49 NKJV).

I like to define destiny using the phrases Jesus used of Himself: I Am (John 6:35), I came to (Matthew 5:17), and I do (John 8:29). It is the amalgamation of these three identifiers that gives us a picture of destiny: the combination of identity, purpose, and action. Jesus also tells us where He is going, which adds to our understanding of destiny: the collective reality of who we are, what we are here for, what we choose to do about it, and the overall goal of where that will lead us.

There is a story in Luke chapter 15 that most know as the story of the prodigal son. The real hero of the story is the father, not because of his morals or his patience, but because of his action. His son (the prodigal) left home and wasted his inheritance. Despite his son's behavior, the father watched and waited, and when he saw his son returning, he took action: he ran out to meet his son. A middle-aged, middle eastern man ran. That simple act of running was uncommon—and even undignified—in that culture.

When I look at the stories that Jesus told, I find myself comparing them to our stories. He was the master communicator and storyteller, but what made Him truly unique was that His story began in heaven and was translated for earth. The stories He told of the Heavenly Father were not the result of Him looking around for ideas on earth of what a father looks like. Rather, He came from the Father and used the landscape in which He was living—the world—to illustrate God's character.

Perhaps the best-known verse in the Bible is not about the character of God or even the thoughts of God, but it is about the doings of God. "For God so loved the world that He gave…" (John 3:16). Sending His son, Jesus, was an act resulting from His heart. He so loved that He was compelled to do something.

Fathers do things. They don't have a set of rules which override emotions, they do things because of their hearts. A father can talk all he likes about his love, but without doing something no one will know the size of his heart. Values without behavior are unconvincing.

Fathers, in their doing, will break rules. This is the result of passion. The father in Luke 15 broke the rules on several occasions, particularly rules pertaining to the accepted culture of the day—the kind of rules that can lead to religious tradition rather than life. The interesting thing about this story is that the elder brother, who is famous for being a rule-keeper, failed his cultural responsibilities, a choice with more serious consequences than breaking rules for love. The story in Luke 15 has been known for a runaway boy and an elder brother who kept the rules, but it should really be most famous for a dad who allowed his heart to cause him to do something.

A father, in his doing, has the power to break religion's grip. Jesus, in one of His most critical statements, accused the Pharisees of being white-walled sepulchers—nicely painted tombs full of dead things. They were fathers who drew a lot of attention to themselves, but they were not doing what they had been created to do and had, therefore, become dead on the inside. Leaders known for lists of rules and regulations create dead religion around themselves. The Pharisees had the ability to look and sound good, but when they were examined more closely they were not alive.

Men and fathers can often feel weighed down by the pressure of being doers. We are accused—sometimes rightfully so—of getting our identity and affirmation from what we do. We can so easily get this wrong, finding our identity in what we do and getting caught up in serving our bosses and masters to the detriment of family. In rectifying that aspect of manhood, we must ensure that we don't create another error by devaluing action. Equally damaging is to think that not doing things is an option.

Mary and Martha are great biblical examples that have often been used to justify a lack of action. We see Jesus rebuke Martha for being in the kitchen while Mary, who has chosen the better role, sits with Jesus. My pastor sometimes breaks the conventional understanding of this story by saying that Martha should have gone to Jesus first, asked Him what she could serve Him, and then gone to prepare the food. The idea behind this interpretation is that the outcome of time spent with Jesus is a desire to take action, and an understanding of what action needs to be taken.

Using the story to justify doing nothing is a misapplication. I, too, have been guilty of busyness and have certainly missed opportunities to sit and listen or rest. But I also know that the result of sitting at Jesus' feet is that I will take action in my life from a new perspective. *Being* is valuable, but it should result in *doing*. One is evidence of the other. True life creates a path which leads to action. Jesus did not come solely to declare who He was. His "I am" statements themselves were all statements declaring His purpose, not just His identity.

Heidi Baker, a missionary and preacher, once said, "Lovers get more done than workers." The key is that lovers still get things done. The result of love is action that demonstrates what is going on in the heart. Jesus asked if He would find faith on the earth when He comes back and we know that faith without works is dead. His question begs a response: will I find people, He is asking, who because of their faith, because of what has happened in their hearts, will be doing things that can be seen and recognized and therefore attributed to faith?

God so loved, that He sent. God is love and out of that He did something. The more we learn to love and be loved, the more productive and effective our actions will be. We must become fathers that take action out of love and unto love. For God so loved the world that He sent Jesus. It doesn't get simpler or more notable than that. God the Father loved us and He chose to do something about it. That's an example worth following.

ACTIVATION QUESTIONS

1. Are there areas in your life in which you are "being" when you need to be "doing," or vice versa? What steps can you take to bring a healthy balance to these areas?

2. What would it look like for your "doing" to come from a place of loving and being loved? How would things change for you and those around you?

9. FATHERS CREATE HOME

"Wait 'til your father gets home!" We've almost all heard that phrase, whether in a movie or out of the mouth of our very own mothers. The phrase, while sometimes humorous or an expression of exasperation, most often conveys a single point: your father will have something to say about this situation. In other words, what we are communicating is the fact that without Dad's approval or input, the scenario is incomplete. The same is true of mothers—when Mom returns home, the conversation can be concluded. Parents bring a sense of completion to the home. In fact, parents create the very culture and the foundation of how we view and experience home.

In the creation of home, it is impossible to separate the male and female roles and contributions. At times we make very clear distinctions between mothers and fathers and their roles in the home, but roles are changing and age-old stereotypes have shifted. Whatever the shift between roles and contributions, the creation and establishing of home—its very existence—is something for which fathers (and mothers) are absolutely vital.

The creation of home, however, is difficult to discuss without an understanding of what this thing is that we call "home." Is it a place? Is it any house in which we dwell? Is home "where the heart is" according to the popular proverb? Home does have something to do with our hearts, but in a much deeper way than home simply being where we long to be in that moment. I lived for fifteen years in another country and had a home there, but I was also aware that the United States wasn't quite home—there was something missing. Bethel Church, on the other hand, was my home. How is that possible?

Home is an address in the heart. It is a sense of shared covering and shared commitment, and a mutual experience of love, support, and encouragement. When all those elements come together in our hearts, we find our home. It is not a location, which is why Sue and I never felt fully at home in the U.S., even though we felt fully at home among our church family. You can live at home and not be "home." Likewise, if home truly is written on our hearts, then with the correct posture we are able to establish home wherever we go. When you become a true son or daughter you can live in less than ideal circumstances, but still receive the best that home has to offer. When you're not a son or daughter you can live in the best home possible and never experience what it means to be home.

In Luke 15, the son makes a decision to return home, knowing that even the least of his father's servants was better off than he was amongst the pigs. In that moment of decision, before he ever took a step toward the physical location of his father's house, the son returned home in his heart. In doing so, he positioned himself to receive the benefits of being home. Without that positioning of the heart, the story may have been quite different. The son would have returned home and his father still would have run to him and showered him with robes and rings and a party. But the boy's experience of home would have been the same as his older brother: he wouldn't have received the grace, the richness of being home.

One day we are all going to be eternally home with our Heavenly Father and experience what that eternal home looks like. While we wait, however, we are meant to model the beauty and glory of relationship, family, and home on earth. This is our role as fathers, but it is also our role as the body of Christ. If we follow Jesus' example and do what we see the Father do (John 5:19), then it is our responsibility to create a sense of home for people in the busyness of life and in the middle of strife, challenges, and tragedies. I remember the first time I went to Bethel Church. Like others before me have expressed, I heard this silent echo of a drumbeat all of my life, and when I arrived at Bethel, I didn't just hear the drums, I met the tribe that carried that beat. It was home because of love, encouragement, support, and commitment to a shared vision. It will forever be an address in my heart.

As parents we have a unique opportunity to show our kids the value and the beauty of home. In our own weakness, we can create a home that is sheltered and stifling, causing our children to flee as soon as they are independent. Or, we can create a home that values authenticity, covering, safety, grace, and unconditional love. This is a home that our children will not only return to, but will be able to find wherever they go in life.

We get to create that, it is what fathers do. We get to create an address in the hearts of our sons and daughters—both natural and spiritual—where they know they're loved and covered, physically, spiritually, and emotionally. We provide them an understanding of shared commitment to a vision, a way of doing life, and a place of safety. We do this through our love, by extending grace and offering a covering. We do this by being authentic and casting a net of safety around our children or those we are raising in the kingdom. We do this by being fathers.

ACTIVATION QUESTIONS

1. What does the concept of "home" mean to you? How easy is it for you to experience home?

2. Ask God if there is any place in you that hasn't yet experienced what it is to be home. What does He want to tell you about it?

10. FATHERS MODEL AUTHENTICITY

Counterfeits are everywhere, and in today's society, that doesn't just apply to the Rolexes on Revolution Street in Tijuana anymore. The word "fake" is thrown around to describe more than just art or knock-off retail items. Fake hits us every time we open our computers or look at our phones—we even use it to describe the news. In a world of social media, where we can share what we consider to be the best aspects of our lives and selves, we are actually more bombarded with inauthenticity than ever. While it is everywhere we turn today, fake is not a new concept. Jesus challenged the Pharisees on this topic, saying, "For you are like whitewashed tombs which indeed appear beautiful outwardly, but inside are full of dead men's bones and all uncleanness" (Matthew 23:27 NKJV).

Authenticity is an important aspect of creating home. Without it, families (and churches) will raise orphans rather than sons and daughters. Authenticity breeds trust, and with trust we can build together, we can share a vision—a key aspect of home. Without trust, we build our own kingdoms.

The model of authenticity starts by recognizing our strengths, our weaknesses, and our failures. But it doesn't end there. When we fail or make mistakes, authenticity comes from acknowledging those mistakes and then overcoming them. Fathers aren't afraid to show weakness. They create an environment where it is okay to say, "I messed up," or "I failed." Fathers provide a safe place to admit defeat and then learn to overcome with victory, and they do this by living that way themselves.

If being real is not allowed in the home, then we are preparing ourselves for struggle. Authenticity is not something we will learn from the world. One day our children are going to face the same situations we have faced, and if they have seen authenticity modeled, it will provide them the strength and wisdom to approach their lives with that same authenticity. In a world where perfection is idolized and imperfection criticized, it is essential that we, as fathers and mothers, demonstrate authenticity to those around us. It doesn't take much. Admit when you bought the wrong car/house/cereal/toothpaste. Don't be afraid to acknowledge a misunderstanding, or fear and insecurity. Allow your kids to watch you navigate the nuances of making decisions as an adult. And through you, they will learn the difference between authenticity and whitewashed walls. They will recognize home as a place where truth is valued and trust is a shared commodity.

ACTIVATION QUESTIONS

1. How authentically are you letting yourself live in front of your own family, your close friends, your team, and your church?

2. Living authentically breeds trust. How can you cultivate trust by living more authentically?

11. FATHERS LOVE UNCONDITIONALLY

Billy Graham's daughter, Ruth, spoke at his funeral and told her story of divorce after twenty-one years of marriage, and then a rapid remarriage against the advice of her family. Almost instantly regretting her second marriage, she fled to her parents, seeking their support.

What was I going to do? I wanted to go talk to my mother and father. It was a two-day drive. Questions swirled in my mind. What was I going to say to Daddy? What was I going to say to Mother? What was I going to say to my children? I'd been such a failure. What were they going to say to me? "We're tired of fooling with you." "We told you not to do it." "You've embarrassed us." Let me tell you. You women will understand. You don't want to embarrass your father. You really don't want to embarrass Billy Graham. And many of you know that we live on the side of a mountain, and as I wound myself up the mountain I rounded the last bend in my father's driveway, and my father was standing there waiting for me. As I got out of the car he wrapped his arms around me, and he said, "Welcome home." There was no shame. There was no blame. There was no condemnation, just unconditional love.

The worst case scenario for a father is to watch his kids going in another direction or living life in a completely different way than they were raised to live. But the absolute truth is unconditional love. I often thought about the "what-ifs" when I was working in prisons. What if my son found his way into prison? What if my son found himself in a moral lifestyle that we didn't agree with? Even when we are unprepared for them, these types of circumstances pull the best out of us as fathers and present us with an opportunity to love unconditionally. It may not happen immediately; there might be anger or rejection before there is love. However, the goal is, and always will be, to love. The goal is for every child to know there is a father waiting for them to come home so he can offer them a robe, ring, sandals, and a party. They might have completely forgotten about that father, but we need to model a home where we are the ones awaiting our child's knock on the door, for just one glimpse of their eye.

My wife has taught me this principle more than anyone else. She taught me three valuable truths about my relationship with my sons: they will always be my sons, I will always love them, they need to know that they are loved by me. In fact, if my wife has anything to do with it, I will spend very little time focused on what I might consider to be my sons' weaknesses or detrimental behaviors. Just like Ruth Graham's story, by the time a child grows up into a young adult and chooses a lifestyle that is completely different to that which was modeled in the home, they already know what their parents are going to think. They don't need disapproval, they already know you disapprove. They just need to feel their parents' unconditional love for them.

The ability to love regardless of the circumstances can be an incredible challenge for all of us. The key is valuing the relationship above the circumstance, or even above our beliefs. Our Heavenly Father loves us unconditionally. Our assignment is to reveal the Father, which means to love unconditionally. We may mess up, and that is okay. What is important is that we keep trying to be fathers who love unconditionally. The embrace of a father creates an imprint in our impressionable minds from an early age, an imprint that teaches us that we are fully and unconditionally loved because we have experienced it in the flesh. That is a home, and a father, worth returning to. Maybe that is why Paul said that out of faith, hope, and love, the greatest is love (1 Corinthians 13:13). The all-encompassing, the biggest, the most eternal, the most important thing we have to offer, is love.

ACTIVATION QUESTIONS

1. Think back over your life—where have you experienced or witnessed unconditional love? What thoughts or feelings did those situations provoke in you?

2. What are your beliefs around how your Heavenly Father loves you? Ask Him whether there are any lies you are believing in this area. What truth does He want to replace those lies with?

12. FATHERS PROVIDE COVERING

"Covering" is a word we often hear spoken around the church. It can be a contentious subject. After all, it is not directly the language of the Bible. Yet, we do see that Paul sent Timothy (1 Corinthians 4:17, 1 Thessalonians 3:2), which could be interpreted as Timothy being covered by his father, Paul. This was not a covering expressed through control, but instead it was one of a proud, loving dad, confident in the exploits of his son and his son's ability to represent him as a father.

Sometimes we can be tempted to reject covering because we have been hurt by a negative expression of what was meant for good. Our experience of error or pain shouldn't mean that we throw aside the concept entirely. Covering that is imposed without relationship is more likely to carry with it elements of control. In reality, covering should make us think of the protection and blessing of a father or mother.

Here is how I like to illustrate covering: as a father, I have the ability to hand out umbrellas. Whether you use the umbrella is up to you. If I insist on holding the umbrella over your head (if my covering comes with control), you get poked, you can't see where you're going, and you still get wet. If I give you an umbrella (if my covering comes with release), you won't hurt your head, you can see where you're going, and you won't get wet.

Covering is not an agreement to a set of rules. It is not alignment over doctrine or paying fees, although all of those things have their place. Instead, I am covered when I allow myself to be commissioned to carry out the vision of a father or mother. If I position my heart as a son toward my parents, I will receive from them as I honor their lives and teachings. In this way, I try to live with my heart available to receive heaven through heaven's representatives. I am free to choose and to reposition my heart if at any point they decide not to represent Christ. That, however, does not give me license to criticize or to stop loving them even if I step away from their covering.

When we position ourselves under the example and blessing (umbrella) of a father, then we are able to access what we need in different scenarios of life. In the early, vulnerable years of life, the mother and father cover, protect, nurture, feed, and keep their children warm. They have a high level of control—they hold the umbrella. In this stage, parents offer a protective and controlling covering. When the children are grown, they get to choose if they want to draw on their family's strength, help, support, and advice. When they are older, they learn how to use the umbrella themselves.

Covering is also to do with the family line. Covering is the blessing that comes down to us like Jacob's blessing passed down to his sons. After 412 years of slavery, Israel still knew who they were because of the power of a father's blessing. The covering or blessing of a father will take you through whatever challenge, crisis, or oppression comes your way. Covering is words of affirmation from a father. It is the lifestyle of obedience or prayer that a father has lived. Once your son has seen the way his father lives his life, then when he faces a similar situation, he will get his umbrella out and walk through that situation the way that his father would.

Fathers provide the umbrella of covering and pass on all of the advantages of that covering to their children, who, as they grow up, decide how they are going to use it. Whatever their decision, the covering remains available, something for our children to grab hold of when they recognize its purpose and blessing.

ACTIVATION QUESTIONS

1. Has your experience of covering been positive or negative? If negative, is there anyone you need to forgive?

2. Are there any inner vows you have made that are stopping you from engaging in healthy relationships with fathers and mothers in your life? Ask your Heavenly Father what He wants to tell you about this area.

13. FATHERS PROVIDE SAFETY

While visiting Sao Paulo, Brazil, I had the pleasure of being driven around by a young man named Titus. As I opened the door to his Chevy for the first time, I stopped suddenly and said, "Oh my, what's up with this car?" "It's armored," he replied. I was baffled. It costs approximately $25,000 to armor a car. So of course, I couldn't help but ask him why his car was armored, and he said, "I was shot a few years ago, and my dad said all his kids were going to have armored cars even if it costs another $25,000 to armor them and put bullet proof glass in them." His story was absolutely incredible. The armoring itself was a wonder—the car was basically a small tank. All I could think while we drove through the city in his Chevy-turned-tank was, "Fathers provide safety." That is exactly what Titus' dad did—he decided his child's safety was more than worth the cost of an armored car.

While Titus' situation was unique, it illustrates God's heart to provide safety for His sons and daughters. What that looks like changes as children grow up. In the very early days of life and childhood, we are intent on keeping our children completely and utterly out of harm's way. Gradually, we grow more lenient and let our kids learn responsibility and, in many ways, how to manage their own safety. This gradual progression is beautifully illustrated in nature with tiny baby ducklings or goslings. When they're very little and liable to get hurt, the parents stay close beside their babies. As they grow, they allow the ducklings just enough room to wander while clearly signaling to them, and any apparent enemy, that they are near and will protect their offspring. Safety is provided in the context of introducing the tiny ducklings to the world and gradually extending their freedom, all while teaching them how to feed and fend for themselves. Fathers do the same. We provide for our children and keep them safe until they are able to protect themselves. Gradually, we release them to find their own way, while always providing a safe home and a safe heart for them to return to. And, as Titus' story shows, a father's heart to keep his kids protected lasts for a lifetime.

ACTIVATION QUESTIONS

1. Where does your safety come from? How do you experience the safety God provides for you?

2. How do you/can you provide safety for your own sons and daughters, natural and spiritual?

14. FATHERS GIVE GRACE FOR THE JOURNEY

My family, especially my youngest son, will often joke, "It's all part of the journey, Dad." That's more than a phrase, it is part of the culture of our family. When life throws us something unexpected, something challenging, or just the normal day-to-day issues that need to be dealt with, we laugh and remind each other that we are on another journey. Not all journeys begin with grace, but as we live and walk out the challenges in front of us, the grace we develop extends to the next generation. In this way we pass on grace for their individual journeys. What does this look like? My book about my journey through prostate cancer, *Kisses from a Good God*, was written with the hope of extending grace. My goal was to share my journey in order to pass on grace to someone else for their own battle, letting them know that they, too, could experience kisses from a good God.

Fathers have already done a lot of the journey. They are further down the road in many of life's experiences and they've been there before, making it easier for those who follow behind them. One of the prophetic words over my family was that we would all live in the same area again. We didn't see how that would happen when that word was given. Just a short time later, however, Sue and I moved back to the UK to be near one of our sons and his family, but in return we left our other son and his wife in America. Amazingly, not long after that, our children in America told us they had also decided to move back to the UK.

Because Sue and I had already made that transition, we were able to help them in their own transition—we were able to give them grace for the same journey we had made.

Giving grace for the journey doesn't look like control—a distinction that is worth mentioning. The mistake we sometimes make as fathers is to expect our children to walk out the journey exactly as we did. The more powerful lesson we can teach our children is not exactly how to walk through life, but how to walk through life understanding grace and God's goodness. This is what we have the opportunity to tell our children: "I'm not sure how it's going to work out, I'm not going to tell you how it's going to work out, but I am going to tell you that there's grace for the journey. I'm going to tell you that my story is that He came through for me."

ACTIVATION QUESTIONS

1. Where in your current journey could you do with more grace? Is there a testimony, biography, or Bible passage you could read that tells the story of someone in a similar situation who God carried through?

2. What unique situations have you been through that have given you the ability to give grace to others on the same journey?

15. FATHERS GIVE IDENTITY

It is now over forty-five years since I heard my father say my name, the name he gave me when I was born. Naming me was his first act of giving me identity. I really enjoy the efforts that so many parents make in choosing their child's first name, or Christian name. Names are packed with meaning. Some have references to biblical names, others have rich cultural meanings or represent loved ones who are no longer with us. Names give us our first understanding of identity—consider how many times our names are spoken each day. Knowing that "Death and life are in the power of the tongue" (Proverbs 18:21), then what power there must be in the simple act of naming our children.

Yet, for all of the effort we go to in giving our children names that have meaning and purpose, it can be so easily undone by calling them negative names. In fact the best of names will not withstand the negative name-calling of an abusive upbringing. How tragic it must be for those who grow up with unhealthy identities and associations. Just as easily as encouragement and blessing can form our identity, negative behavior or family history can form an unhealthy identity. Fathers carry the power to give identity, not just to their children, but to their entire family.

The surname is equally significant in carrying identity to your family. Imagine for a moment being raised in a family where the father's reputation was the worst in the community. Nobody would expect the children to amount to anything.

Failures would be accepted as unavoidable if the family name was associated with failure. Without the expression of healthy identity within the family, the reputation created by previous generations can harm the generations to come. If that is true in the negative, consider the reverse. A family name to live up to, encouragement at every turn, freedom to take the best of the identity given and mold it to the unique gifts, abilities, and desires of the child. How different to have a reputation following them that expected success and the display of good character.

Just as I consider the fact that I haven't heard my father say my name in so many years, I have often wondered what being a Manwaring meant to him. He bore that name as part of a team designing bombs in the Second World War and as a young officer collecting intelligence in Germany. I like to think he was proud to be a Manwaring. I have now passed that name to two sons, two grandsons, and, as is common through marriage, to my wife. For me, it represents the identity I have helped provide to my family. Prior to moving back to the UK, our family was separated for fifteen years, one son living in the UK and the other with us in the USA. We developed ways of coping with goodbyes by avoiding certain actions at airports. Long hugs at airports and telling my boys I'm proud of them were not allowed. Actually, we considered them illegal activities. We dealt with the emotion of goodbyes in private, but in the airport we just reminded ourselves that "We are the Manwarings." That was our identity as a family.

Of course, identity is more than just a name. In whatever way a child derives his or her surname, the giving of inner identity is abundantly more important. Even though it was over thirty years ago, I remember the day my aging grandfather called me a "good man." Through all of the tests and trials of life, that moment has lived in my memory. How we are known will have the greatest of effects on us for bad and for good. Who we tell our children they are will directly affect who they become.

Fathers give identity. We do this by giving names, through encouragement, and by association. We do it in the highs of life and the lows of life. Our words do not allow the lowest moments, or even the successes of life to define identity. Our family names will live on, but so will the identity given by experience, encouragement, and reputation. It is right to raise our kids with an identity of which they can be proud.

ACTIVATION QUESTIONS

1. This chapter describes the effect on our identity of name-calling (good and bad) as we grow up. What was your experience in this area? Ask God if there are any names you were called that are still affecting your identity. If there are, forgive those involved, break off the negative effects, and ask God what name He calls you by. How can you reinforce this new identity in your day-to-day life?

2. How can you sow life into those around you through being intentional about your words and how you treat people?

16. FATHERS HELP THEIR CHILDREN DISCOVER WHAT THEY LOVE

"Delight yourself in the Lord, And He will give you the desires of your heart" (Psalm 37:4). The Heavenly Father gives us the desires of our hearts, and He also *gives* us the desires of our hearts. That is, He put the desires in our hearts, but then He gives us opportunities to see those desires fulfilled. This is one of the great keys of being fathers: to give our children permission to discover what they love and help them to fulfill that passion. I remember when our oldest grandson was about eighteen months old, he said to me, "Blue and green are my favorite colors. I love blue and green." I wanted to say, "Who told you?" I thought surely he was too young to come to that conclusion on his own. But he wasn't. He had been given an environment in which he could explore his love for different things. I like to think I did the best I possibly could with my sons, but now I get to see the next generation experience new opportunities and environments that allow them to make genuine choices.

Many of us embark on careers and education without exploring our likes and desires. We build life based on the discovery of what we can do or deliver. For some of us, if we are fortunate, we embark on our career path from a place of passion. However, for those of us who haven't explored our passion or the desires of our heart, we instead depend on our basic abilities to make a living. For this group of people, it is only later—whether through an encounter with God or a mid-life crisis—that we begin to dream and perhaps discover a previously hidden passion. The pattern we live out is to learn, design the life we want, and deliver our skill to the world in order to live the life we designed. But what if life is supposed to begin, rather, with a discovery of what we love? What if fathers are supposed to correct the journey? How wonderful it would be if we started life with discovery of our passions, dream about what life could be, then design that life and deliver it.

God gives us the desires of our hearts, and as fathers we get to help our children unfold those desires. How is this done? I believe Psalm 27:4 is part of the journey: "One thing I have desired of the Lord, That will I seek: That I may dwell in the house of the Lord All the days of my life, To behold the beauty of the Lord…" (NKJV). As we behold His beauty we come alive to the desires He has placed in us. This is amplified even further by Song of Solomon 4:9, "You have stolen my heart with one glance of your eyes" (NIV). One look at God's beauty and we cannot help but beat with the passion He has given us. Fathers create an environment in which their children have the opportunity to behold God's beauty and discover their unique purpose. We create an environment in which children can explore the desires of their hearts.

Exploring our desires is made more accessible in an environment of abundance. I am not referring to an abundance of finances, but rather a mindset that there is more than enough room for sons and daughters to discover what they love. I remember reading through Stephen M.R. Covey's book *The Speed of Trust*, and learning about the importance of choosing abundance. Stephen writes, "The important thing to understand is this: abundance is a choice, abundance is a mindset and a way of being and becoming. It is a foundational element in improving intent, which will make us more credible and believable with others. When I'm in the middle of a negotiation do I really believe that it's possible to come up with a solution that will provide benefit to both sides?" (Pages 88-89).

How do we know if we have created an environment of abundance, making room for our children to explore what they love? Ask yourself these questions: Are there limits on recognition and on love in my home? Is there room for other people to see things differently? Is there room for another opinion, a different choice, or is there only one "right" answer on this subject? Abundance means there is room for more than one viewpoint or one thought. It also means that there are not any limits on emotion, on being affirmed, encouraged, or recognized. God did not give the world a limited amount of talents or skills. There is more than enough for everyone. As we become comfortable with this idea, it will allow us to create a place where our children can discover what they love in a culture of abundance that allows for choice.

ACTIVATION QUESTIONS

1. Are there limits on recognition and on love in your home? Is there room for other people to see things differently? Is there room for another opinion, a different choice, or is there only one "right" answer on a subject? What do your answers reveal about your current ability to help your sons and daughters to discover what they love?

2. How was your journey growing up? Did you get the chance to discover what you love?

For more help on this journey, check out Paul's blog "PERSONAL DISCOVERY SERIES: PART 1: P IS FOR PASSION" at his website paulmanwaring.com, which has practical steps for starting this journey of discovery.

17. FATHERS BELIEVE IN THEIR CHILDREN

Some time ago, Banning Liebscher, pastor of Jesus Culture in Sacramento, California, preached a message and said, "You know, kids, they believe they're going to be astronauts… they believe they're going to win whatever trophy it is. They believe in it! And you know, it's for us as parents to run with those beliefs. And to believe in our kids (with them)." Belief in someone or something is an act of trust. When someone believes in you, they are saying, among other things, that they trust you. The same is true of a father. Belief in your child is not only trust, but also a sentiment that removes doubt and builds confidence. I don't expect that Jesus suffered from doubt, but there is a relationship between receiving the Father's affirmation and the commencement of His public ministry. God spoke over Him, "This is My beloved Son, in whom I am well pleased" (Matthew 3:17), and those words launched Jesus into His ministry on earth. Jesus, who was fully God and fully man, needed His father's trust. As our sons and daughters embark on their life journeys there is, perhaps, no greater endorsement than the affirmation that comes from a father.

I can remember scenarios during my teenage years when, in the absence of my father, I couldn't access a voice of encouragement or belief in my head. I found myself doing the best I could, being responsible as best I could, but being left to work out my successes and failures on my own. My mother offered her support and did it exceptionally well, but as a young man I knew that there was something missing. In recent years, I have been privileged to receive, and be guided by some incredibly accurate prophetic words. The journey of seeing those words fulfilled in my life has greatly compensated for the lack of fatherly belief in my life. As a personal revelation or a prophetic word has come to pass, I have seen that, although I may sometimes doubt, my Heavenly Father believes in me enough to encourage me through others.

Lacking support from a father in my adolescent years gave me an entirely different perspective toward the men I encountered as a prison manager. While working in a young offenders prison, I began to value the role of a father-figure in providing belief and trust, even toward those who aren't making good life choices. At one point, I interviewed 300 boys coming into my prison. I purposefully chose not to talk to them about their crime, but rather about their best life experiences and their future hopes and dreams. Everyone needs to feel that they are believed in, even if there doesn't seem to be something obvious to affirm in their lives. We all have values and dreams, and we all need a father to tell us that we are loved, we are valued, and we are capable of great things. When things don't seem easy or children aren't living to their potential, fathers ask questions. We discover the hopes and dreams of our children, eradicate doubt through affirmation, and encourage them toward who they are meant to be.

ACTIVATION QUESTIONS

1. Think back to when someone you respected believed in you. What effect did it have on you? How can you encourage others in the same way?

2. How do you access your Heavenly Father's voice of encouragement? How does it change things knowing that Father God believes in you?

18. FATHERS CELEBRATE VICTORIES AND ESTABLISH MEMORIALS

All throughout scripture the people of Israel demonstrate the beauty of building memorials—reminders of what God had done for them. They built memorials of stones when they crossed over the Jordan, each aspect of the tabernacle and the temple was a memorial, even the engraved stones that sat on the ephod that Aaron wore were a memorial to the sons of Israel (Exodus 28:12). The Israelites taught us the value of celebrating and memorializing what God has done in and through our lives. As fathers, we have the privilege of teaching our children and those around us this same value—reminding ourselves and the world of what God has done.

I believe fathers almost innately celebrate victories by establishing memorials. It simply looks different in our modern world. After moving to the United States, it was an uphill struggle to obtain a religious worker's visa which would allow us to stay in Redding, and allow me to work at Bethel Church. When the visa finally came through, we bought a TV, our memorial to God's faithfulness and our perseverance. It was a great memorial because we would look at it every day and we all knew what it was for. A memorial of God's goodness doesn't have to be a pile of stones; it can be a nice, grey Sony in the corner. What is most important is that we demonstrate the value of remembering what God has done for us.

Proverbs 22:28 reads, "Do not remove the ancient landmark, which your fathers have set" (NKJV). Every small victory is part of a bigger family-wide victory. Being able to refer back to those memorial stones is important as we raise the next generation. When they face their battle, they can look back and say, "God did it before and He will do it again." This is the power of the testimony lived out. As we find ways of celebrating victories and establishing memorials, we are writing the family story that will be passed down through the generations. Families sit around the meal table and share stories of how they won a victory or how God came through for them, and it is important that we teach our children to remember and pass on those stories.

We often create memorials when there is something to celebrate, but celebration is not based on achievement alone. There are times when success is our reason for celebrating, but fathers love unconditionally, and they celebrate and throw parties even when their kids don't deserve it. In Luke 15, the father killed the fatted calf and hosted a party not because his son deserved it, but because his son was alive. "For this son of mine was dead and has come to life again; he was lost and has been found" (Luke 15:24). This is the centerpiece of the Christian faith, the gospel message. None of us deserve to be celebrated by the standards of righteousness, but we are made righteous and celebrated because of what Jesus did for us. Likewise, fathers celebrate in the good times when things go well by creating memorials, and they celebrate in the bad times because relationship is always worth celebrating.

ACTIVATION QUESTIONS

1. Is celebration a part of your life? Why/why not?

2. What memorial stones do you have in your life? What could you do to celebrate an aspect of God's faithfulness in your life in this season?

19. FATHERS RAISE FAVORITES

A few years ago I took a phone call with a very experienced church leader who had questions about the way in which church teams make decisions about pay rates. It was one of those conversations where I learned more than the person asking the questions. I had some answers to the practical side of how we do things, but it very soon began to transition to a conversation about why we do things the way we do, particularly as it pertains to things that might not seem fair.

Let me paint a few scenarios: In the desire to serve a ministry, people are willing to work for less. Single people tend to be recruited for less pay than those with families, and in some cases, married women will also work for less pay if their families are not dependent solely on their income. Both scenarios could easily be challenged, and validly so, but they are the reality of many growing ministries eager to make a difference with limited resources. This was, in essence, the root of my conversation with this pastor. So how, he asked, do we justify this reality, at least until there is a more equitable system?

I happen to know two of this pastor's sons; they are both successful in their own right but they are different in what they do, what they love, and what they need. I asked him if he loved his sons equally and also whether each of them would feel that they are his favorite. He told me that he thought they would. I went on to ask whether he treated them both the same. After a brief pause, he said that he does not, he treats them differently.

After that, we didn't need to talk about pay scales and fairness and equality, but about the beauty of raising favorites.

We often make the mistake of attributing the expression of favor as a comparison: if one person is a favorite, then everyone else is not. Not long ago it was common to hear people say, "I'm God's favorite," particularly in an environment like Bethel's School of Ministry, where students are on a journey of discovering their identity. It is a wonderful perspective in the context of identity and removed from the context of comparison. However, when spoken or believed from a place of insecurity or an orphan mindset, this sentiment can manifest as someone considering themselves more important than others. It can even be perceived as carrying an attitude that a person can do no wrong.

The God we love and serve, our Father, Dad or Papa doesn't have one favorite, we are all His favorites and that favor is not to be confused with preferential treatment. The examples of favor in the Bible, especially in the Old Testament, were of favor given for the benefit of someone else. We see this beautifully portrayed in Genesis 50, at the time of Jacob's death. Joseph approached Pharaoh's court to ask for permission to leave Egypt to bury his father in Canaan, saying, "If now I have found favor in your eyes" (Genesis 50:4). Amazingly Pharaoh not only gave permission, but also mourned extravagantly with Joseph and his family.

Favor in the New Testament is often translated from the greek "caris"—from which we get the word charismatic—which is often translated as grace. Grace, of course, is not expressed from heaven in the context of comparison. It is something we all receive freely. In fact, the idea of giving and receiving of gifts is much more relatable to our experience of our Father in heaven. He is a gift-giver and He gives us gifts from a place of knowledge: knowing us and knowing the desires of our hearts. He doesn't give equally all the time, but He gives according to who we are. I would much rather receive a gift of lesser value representing the Father's knowledge of me than a more expensive gift that was unconnected to my identity, passions, or season of life. Being known and receiving that expression is the pattern of the one who raises favorites.

This is an important foundation for things fathers do. The most valuable things fathers do will not be monetary but will flow from relationship, from knowing our children. We give identity through creating an environment where children can discover what they love, by believing in our children, teaching them to celebrate and remember, and raising favorites. We raise favorites not by treating everyone the same, but by treating individuals according to their gifting, needs, identity, and the season of their lives. We raise favorites by treating them according to who they are. And we encourage them to know their unique identity.

ACTIVATION QUESTIONS

1. In what ways have you felt God's favor on you and on your life?

2. Consider those in your immediate circle. What would it look like to treat each one of them as a "favorite"?

20. FATHERS FOSTER GROWTH

Growth is an interesting concept, an experience that can be difficult to gauge if we are not on the outside, looking in. Sometimes we don't notice our own growth and maturing as it is happening, but we can see it so clearly in those around us. Fathers foster growth in their children, particularly emotional maturity, compassion, responsibility, and their capacity to pursue dreams and new opportunities. From the outside, it is easier for us, as fathers, to see our children's strengths and weaknesses, their unique and natural talents, and their passions. Sometimes we think it is only the mother's role to nurture, but it is also the father's role to nurture our children's natural gifting, creating opportunities and a wider perspective from which they can grow and become who they are meant to be.

Fostering and creating growth isn't just about teaching our children how to grow and mature, but creating a place where truth and grace can prevail. For example, when children know that they are loved, the goals and targets they choose to pursue in life come from a place of love, rather than fear or doubt. Jesus was full of grace and truth, and from that place He challenged His disciples toward growth. Grace must come first; it softens the heart to receive the truth, where truth alone could harden the heart and prevent you from receiving grace. When fathers create an environment of grace, it is a safe place for parents to love, teach truth, and challenge their children. In this way we grow as fathers and our children grow in maturity.

Modeling how we go through tough situations is another way of fostering growth. The current manager of the England national soccer team, for example, is famous for missing a penalty, which saw England kicked out of Euro '96. This past World Cup, he walked his team through winning a very important match during a penalty shootout—the very thing that caused him and the country so much disappointment twenty-two years before. He has been fathering his players and using his tough season to nurture growth in them. We can sometimes be afraid of how hard situations will affect our children, but we all know that we grow the most during the tough seasons of life. If I model that growth to my children, then when they come to the tough seasons of life they will know that regardless of the situation, it will help them to grow.

Jesus taught us to lead our children even farther than we have gone, not just helping them grow, but teaching them how to walk in growth on their own. When I was growing up, parents would try to keep their children away from Hollywood so that they wouldn't be polluted by Hollywood culture. Today, we are a generation that will send our children into the very cultures we avoided because we believe that they will influence those cultures for good. As we give freedom and permission for them to go further than we have and take on the challenges of life, we encourage and celebrate growth.

ACTIVATION QUESTIONS

1. We can often become discouraged as we look at our own progress and growth, particularly if we start comparing ourselves to others. If you struggle with this, take a moment to ask God how He sees you. What does He think of how you're doing?

2. What have been the triggers for the seasons of rapid growth in your life?

21. FATHERS MODEL HOW TO COPE

My training as a psychiatric nurse began in the East End of London. There are many causes of mental illness and the East End of London was an area well known for studies of the effects of environment on mental health. In those days I created a definition for myself of mental health: it is the ability to be responsible for our behavior, despite conflicting emotions (or voices) in our minds. While some mental illness will not be related to this, the ability to show emotions and be responsible for those emotions is a vital part of our life experience. Our ability to display emotions in a healthy way equips us for all that life may deliver to us. Emotions that are locked up, bottled, and left to fester and accumulate will find their way out eventually, causing explosions of unruled grief, loss, or anger.

I love the Psalms, perhaps mostly because they are a display of emotions: the good, the bad, and even the ugly. There is no emotion or expression of emotion that our Heavenly Father cannot handle, and this should be the guide for fathers—demonstrating how to handle success and failure, loss and gain. As fathers, we have an opportunity to display an array of emotions and circumstances against the backdrop of what really matters in life. We show our children what it looks like to take responsibility for our feelings in the midst of circumstances that are the opposite of what we pray or hope for. With our lives, we demonstrate that we believe in God's ability to redeem, that He wastes nothing and He gets us ready.

As a prison governor, I once had a visit from the Chief Inspector of Prisons. While it is nerve-racking to experience that level of inspection, I am grateful for the experience because it gave me an opportunity to show my sons the importance of integrity and walking out the more intense aspects of leadership. Recently, one of my sons had the School Authority visit his school and run inspections. I was reminded of the fact that he watched me walk through that very experience and had a point of reference for coping with the stress of an inspection. As we walk out our journey as fathers, dealing with what life throws at us in a healthy way, we show our sons and daughters how to do the same. We get to teach them that they can depend on God as we have depended on God. This in itself is a type of promotion, not just in terms of movement to a higher position or rank. Promotion is also forward motion. In moving our children forward we are helping them to grow upward too.

ACTIVATION QUESTIONS

1. The display of healthy emotion is vital for the healthy development of our children. Did you get to see this as you were growing up? How did your experiences craft your belief systems in this area?

2. What does "healthy emotion" look like to you?

22. FATHERS DEMONSTRATE AN ATTITUDE OF THANKFULNESS

Teaching our children to cope with the conflicting emotions of life also means teaching them thankfulness. Too often we fall into self-pity, demonstrating a focus on what we don't have, rather than what we do have. Our job as fathers is to eradicate self-pity and teach, instead, the art of gratitude.

As I write this, I am watching the 2018 World Cup with my sons, and it reminds me of my time in Brazil with my son four years ago. England didn't do so well in that World Cup and even as we watched them lose, it didn't dampen the trip. Our experience was about so much more than watching England win. Luke and I had tickets for an England game that really meant nothing in terms of their standing in the World Cup. They were already going to be eliminated, regardless of the outcome of that game. We could easily have walked into the stadium with an attitude of regret that we missed the games that really mattered. Instead, Luke and I kept looking at each other in awe, saying, "I can't believe we're here!" As we came into the stadium in Brazil, I went off to get a drink and Luke told me he would meet me at our seats. I was in the line to get the drink and suddenly Luke came back to me and said, "I couldn't walk through those doors into an England game in Brazil without you, Dad." I was touched at my son's ability to express gratitude in the midst of what could have, with a different mindset, been a disappointing experience.

Fathers teach their children how to focus on what is available instead of what isn't available. The mindset of gratitude is a valuable skill to learn in coping with the ups and downs of life, and fathers have the influence to pass that skill on to their children. Even if we feel that we are still learning this lesson ourselves, our children watch what we do, how we live, and they will learn from watching us walk out the journey of coping and being thankful.

ACTIVATION QUESTIONS

1. How do you practice and demonstrate thankfulness?

2. How easy is it for you to find things to be thankful for in the midst of less-than-ideal situations?

23. FATHERS SHOW THEIR CHILDREN THE WORLD

Mothers are typically credited with creating an environment where children feel nurtured and loved. Even in the world of inner healing, we communicate the mother's role as creating security within the home and providing comfort, while fathers provide other needed elements of home life. As a father who worked a lot when my sons were young, I struggled with understanding my role in the home and what I was to provide as a father. If Sue was the nurturer, what did I bring?

I spent a season of my life working seventy-five hours a week—a season that was far too long. One Tuesday night, Sue was on the worship team at our church, and I was on call. In fact, I was on call to the prison 24/7. Sue had gone to worship practice and I had the two boys, when a call came through that there was a very serious suicide attempt at my prison. I bundled up my boys and I dumped them at the church on the way to the prison. I felt horrible, thinking that I did a horrible job of creating a safe, comforting home environment. Instead of watching over my boys at home, I left them to do my job. But in that moment, I realized something that has stuck with me to this day. While I was not able to provide a nurturing environment, I instead showed my boys the world. Through that incident and my role as prison manager, my boys were exposed to a wider, sometimes scarier world, in which someone feels desperate enough to attempt suicide. For months after that event, they would ask me how that prisoner was doing. While it was not my intent at the time, their exposure to the world that night taught them a compassion that they both carry to this day.

While this particular event may feel extreme, it is a real-life scenario of what it means for fathers to show our children the world. In the traditional model of home and family, mothers build the home while fathers go off to work. I realize this isn't the case for everyone and is even the opposite for some families. Regardless of whether you have a home where both parents work, or where the mom works and the dad stays at home, the role of the father does not change. He has an opportunity to teach his children his experience of the world. Fathers share stories of people they meet, things they encounter, and how they see the world around them.

A few years ago, I was in Brazil with Sean Feucht, an itinerant minister. As we shared stories and got to know one another, Sean told me about his very first mission trip with his dad. He was twelve years old and they put him in charge of pulling rotten teeth for villagers in the Amazon. I was amazed. His dad took him and showed him the world in a most profound way. If I consider Sean now, I can see that he is who he is because of that experience. The world his father showed him embedded itself deep into his heart and has never left him. We don't all have that same upbringing or such intense experiences, but we certainly all have the opportunity to show our kids the world in a way that will profoundly impact them.

ACTIVATION QUESTIONS

1. In what ways did you get a glimpse into the world of your parents as you were growing up? How did it shape who you are today?

2. What experiences and windows into the world does your life afford you? How are you inviting your children into the world as you know it?

24. FATHERS TEACH RESPONSIBILITY

As fathers, we bear burdens for our children. A five-year-old, for instance, doesn't need to know that their parents are struggling to pay the mortgage. There are a lot of things that parents and families deal with, aspects of adult life, that aren't a child's job to carry—at least not until they are old enough to learn to carry their own responsibilities. Even in Jesus' life, God let Him grow up to be a man before He sent Him out. As fathers we need to do the same.

I often hear an idea tossed around that "adulting" is hard. That is, being an adult and carrying a certain level of responsibility is challenging. I like to think that if we do our job as fathers in teaching our children what responsibility looks like, maybe "adulting" wouldn't be so hard for this and the next generation. It is true that today's youth and young adults face challenges, financially and socially, that my generation never had to face. The economy has changed, the internet has become a profound part of our daily lives, and social media has presented an element of social life that I didn't deal with growing up. Regardless of the changes in society, I still had an opportunity to teach my boys how to live responsibly: how to pay bills, how to be a good employee, and how to take responsibility for their actions.

Similar to teaching our children how to cope, fathers teach them what it means to be a responsible human being. As with everything we teach and learn, this looks different through various lenses and worldviews. For some, responsibility looks like taking care of the environment, for others it is avoiding debt, and still others will see responsibility as denying a dream in order to provide for a family. Regardless of what this means, children learn to understand responsibility by watching their fathers and their mothers navigate their own adult experiences. As we learn to live out our purpose on this earth and walk in responsibility to our calling as children of God, so too will our children. Just as Jesus, at the right moment, stepped into His responsibility as God's sacrifice to the world, we can teach our children how to carry their role, their calling, their destiny, and their identity into adulthood.

ACTIVATION QUESTIONS

1. What does responsibility mean to you?

2. How do you determine when a son or daughter is ready for more responsibility? How does this compare to your experience of the way your Heavenly Father has fathered you in the area of increased responsibility?

25. FATHERS CREATE OPPORTUNITIES

Four hundred years ago it was obvious that if my name was Smith, I would get a job as a blacksmith in my father's shop. In other words, my father's identity and occupation would create an opportunity for me. That was the way the world worked. It doesn't work that way anymore, but it is still our job as fathers to create opportunity for our children. What does that look like in today's society? I have wrestled with this idea, particularly as it pertains to ministry, and even business. I have watched ministry families create opportunities for their kids and thought it was nepotism. And there is nepotism at times—I get it. But I also believe that the enemy wants us to criticize such instances, calling it nepotism, fearing nepotism, because it will prevent us from doing what we're meant to do: create opportunities for our children.

Bill Johnson says that he intentionally creates opportunities for his kids because they paid a price growing up with a dad in ministry. It's the same with Sean Feucht—his father created opportunities for him that became the foundation for his ministry. He is changing the world because his dad created opportunities.

Earlier this year, I had a meeting at a large broadcasting network. The meeting had been delayed almost a year, the timing of which I didn't understand until later. As it turned out, my son had just moved back to the UK, and as he has a passion for television studios and filming, I asked permission to bring him along to the meeting. In the course of the afternoon, the director asked my son what he was doing and when he said he was looking for a job, they offered him a job at their network. I didn't take my son that day with the intention of getting him a job, but as a father, I had a right to create an opportunity for him—even if the end result was beyond my influence. It is legal to find those opportunities and to create those opportunities for our kids.

We don't just create opportunities in the realm of work, either. My favorite times with both my sons are when they discover something new that brings them life. In the case of my eldest son, he developed an appreciation for Jools Holland and his incredible ability on the piano. I wanted to create an opportunity for him to explore his passion, and so I took him to a Jools Holland concert. In fact, we have been to several together. As dads, we can be thinking about how we can create opportunities for our children to meet people who inspire them or participate in activities that bring them joy. Ask yourself, do I have an opportunity to share that will benefit my family? If so, you are released to let your children benefit from the opportunities available to you.

ACTIVATION QUESTIONS

1. Have you withheld from sharing opportunities from your family because of a fear of nepotism?

2. Do you have an opportunity to share that could benefit your family?

26. FATHERS DREAM WITH THEIR CHILDREN

Psalm 126 says, "When the Lord brought back the captive ones of Zion, We were like those who dream." The Psalm declares how the children of Israel were freed from captivity and given freedom to dream again as a nation. In bondage, dreams are diminished, even our ability to dream is subdued. In freedom, not only can we dream again, but we can pursue the dreams to make them a reality. Fathers help their children dream by creating an environment where dreams can thrive.

It is difficult, for instance, for an individual to have their own dream within the confines of an authoritarian or communist regime. The emphasis on regulation and control within these systems does not allow the level of private or entrepreneurial growth that is seen in places like Western Europe and North America. In the United States, it is normal to pursue what is called the "American Dream," where the culture itself provides permission for individuals to not only dream, but see that dream realized. We have the same opportunity within our realm of influence as fathers to build a culture where our children are allowed to dream their own dreams.

It can be difficult creating a culture that we didn't have growing up. It is especially challenging if our children are particularly gifted, or doing something we always wanted to do ourselves. There are far more opportunities today than there were even a decade ago, making it easy for us to think, "I didn't have that, Son," or "I had to work hard for that, so you should too." Despite how hard it may be, we are meant to be joyful when the next generation has opportunities that we never had. We are meant to celebrate that with them. It is powerful when a father recognizes a gift or a talent in his child and blesses that. I watch some people who grow up in homes of freedom, where their gifts and talents are recognized and affirmed. In giving permission to dream, a father gives his children the ability to go into the world secure in their identity. Similar to providing an environment of abundance to explore what we love, fathers provide permission to dream about and pursue what we are good at.

In the Christian culture, the need for permission to dream is particularly felt by those pursuing creative careers or dreams. It has often seemed easy to pursue a creative career outside of the church, but as a church we have not always given permission to our children to use their creative gifts and talents. I often think the reason the church isn't full of great entrepreneurs is because the church didn't create a culture of permission. Instead, religion and control—the opposites of freedom—held people back. As a result we have the Steve Jobs and Richard Bransons of the world filling the earth with the knowledge of the glory of themselves, rather than of God. When I minister to creatives, I like to make this simple declaration over them: "Permission granted." Spiritual permission and emotional consent, particularly from a parent or spiritual father, brings freedom.

Helping our children grow doesn't just happen by creating an environment of permission, but by dreaming along with them. I love watching people come alive when you ask them what their dreams are, and get to share the excitement of those dreams with them. Dreaming doesn't have to be extravagant or particularly spiritual, even just the everyday moments of goals and desires are worth sharing with your children, spiritual or natural. Even if those dreams can't or don't become a reality right away, dreaming together is a journey. When the dreams do become a reality, you get to share in that joy with your children.

In the same way fathers give identity to their children, they also create the very opportunities for their children to grow and expand into their identities. Jesus demonstrated this best, teaching His disciples to grow in truth, while setting them up to continue the journey of growth once He was gone. "And greater works than these he will do, because I go to My Father" (John 14:12). He created such a culture of growth that His disciples would exceed their master. He wasn't intimidated by that and neither should we be intimidated. It is our great joy as fathers to watch our children grow in emotional maturity, in responsibility, compassion, and in opportunity to live out their dreams. The Father is so pleased to give us this responsibility, and in the same way we celebrate the growth of our children, He celebrates our growth as fathers.

ACTIVATION QUESTIONS

1. How healthy are you in the area of dreaming dreams for your own life? What does God want to tell you about the way you dream?

2. Do you feel able to celebrate the successes of your children? Why or why not?

27. FATHERS SERVE

Serving others is often seen as a chore, but it's one of the great pleasures of life to serve our children and to create in them a desire to serve others. Ultimately, if we don't serve our families, we don't serve our children. Jesus said He came to serve, not to be served. What higher example is there than the example of Jesus, our eternal Father? Just before Jesus teaches the Lord's Prayer in scripture, He says, "Your Father knows what [you're going to ask] before you ask Him" (Matthew 6:8, my paraphrase). If my boys call my wife with a request, I can almost always determine what they are calling for just based on the fact that they are calling Sue and not me. The same is true if they call me rather than my wife. Serving our families looks like meeting their needs, and sometimes, it looks like knowing their needs before they speak a word.

In 2001, my wife, youngest son, and I got on a plane and flew to America with only a few suitcases, a couple years' worth of money, and a one-year visa. The decision to leave the UK and travel to America came from a place of service. My wife knew that she needed to be in Redding, and so we went. In serving Sue, I was serving our family and our children, and demonstrating to them the importance of service. I've watched my youngest son, Luke, do the same for his wife. The ability to model service to our children sets them up to learn how to be great servants.

Two things I love to do are to cook and make coffee. Both are hobbies that I, in turn, use to serve my family. I love to share my new recipes with them, or make them that perfect cup of coffee in the morning. It is a delight to shower them with love by providing them with nourishment on a very practical level. It is my way of demonstrating servitude to my family. In Isaiah 9:6, Jesus is given the title "Prince of Peace." The prince is the son of the king and his role is to serve the king and serve the people. A father is also a son. As a son of the King of Kings, I am a prince called to serve the King and the people. Just as Jesus modeled service to us, so must we model it to our children. In doing so we set a bar for our kids, saying "This is what service looks like." We set them up to serve their families as fathers, as sons, and as princes.

I've never been to Wimbledon, which seems almost criminal given that we live so close. There was a Saturday when all of my family went to Wimbledon and I had to work. Fathers do what is right, and sometimes it might cost you. Sometimes as fathers, we create an opportunity for the family in which we can't actually participate. We pay a price to put food on the table and build a future for our families. Our Heavenly Father did this too: He was willing to pay a price for His family by sending His son.

One of the greatest delights as a father is to serve your family with pleasure. It is not a chore or an obligation, it is a great privilege. Our service to our family isn't just financial or in mundane responsibility, but in providing fun opportunities and surprises. Sue and I love creating transatlantic surprises for our family. It's not easy to pull it off, but we've done four, and they are worth it. Luke, our youngest, got James, our eldest, to fly from London to Redding to surprise me when I was in surgery for prostate cancer. A few years ago, we flew Luke to England to surprise James for his thirtieth birthday. James went into a pub for his traditional end-of-term pint, only to discover

Luke leaning against the bar. We showed up at my mother's ninetieth birthday, unbeknownst to her. It should be noted that you have to be a little more careful with surprises at that age. Regardless of what this looks like tangibly, fathers serve their families when it costs them, and they serve their families with fun.

ACTIVATION QUESTIONS

1. How is your relationship with your Heavenly Father? Do you feel that you can ask Him for whatever you need with confidence? If not, what is standing in your way?

2. What are your favorite ways of serving your family?

28. FATHERS MODEL DUTY AND ROYALTY

There has been a lot of talk recently following the royal wedding of Meghan Markle to Prince Harry. A lot of it has been about how much she had to give up to become part of the royal family. But it's not arduous—it is duty. It is about love. She stepped into her new role and duty from a place of love for Prince Harry, not out of obligation. The word duty can easily be misunderstood, but in many ways, it sums up the service of a father to his family. It is a word often used to describe the way in which a king or queen serves his or her country and commonwealth. The word duty embraces the cost of service done in joy, while also encompassing the sense of being born into something without choice.

The current Queen of England has served the country and done it incredibly well, even becoming the longest-reigning British monarch. She has carried out a duty because she was born into her role—it was part of her bloodline, destiny, and purpose. I'm sure there are times she wants simply to put her feet up and relax, but royalty serves. In the case of the Pope and the Archbishop of Canterbury, duty and service look slightly different. There are things, I'm sure, that they do not agree with in their denominations. People say, "Well, why are they doing that? And if they don't agree with it why don't they just leave?" These leaders have been given an opportunity to impact history and have great influence. Duty pays a price. Jesus also had a duty and paid the greatest price of them all. Duty is about bloodline, DNA, a destiny, and a purpose. We're not kings in the natural, but we have the opportunity to show what it looks like to be royal, to serve something, and to serve somebody.

As fathers, our duty is to our family, our bloodline, and those who carry our DNA. It is our responsibility to not only fulfill our duty to them, but demonstrate what it looks like to serve from a place of duty rather than obligation. It is not difficult, it just requires that we look at the world through the eyes of a prince, with our hearts set on serving our King and the people He has placed within our "kingdom." We are royalty and we get to share that reality with our children.

ACTIVATION QUESTIONS

1. Do you recognize yourself as a prince called to serve the King and the people? Are there any lies you are believing about your identity as royalty? Ask God what He wants to tell you about this area.

2. In what ways are you modeling duty and royalty to your family?

29. FATHERS GIVE INHERITANCE AND LEAVE A LEGACY

We all desire to give and receive financial inheritance at an appropriate time in our lives, but inheritance and legacy are so much more than financial wealth. I have heard many stories of people who became overnight millionaires due to financial inheritance, and it brought them to ruin. Without the foundational inheritance of Christ, knowing how to love and serve, without experiencing the love of a father and the love of the Father, financial inheritance will not lend itself to legacy. How can we leave a legacy? Understand what it is to be a father, the significance of the role you play, and you will leave a legacy for your family that is more valuable than money.

Fascinatingly, my father was a strategist and a manager. He helped build the bouncing bomb and later ended up working in an establishment for young offenders. He was also a lay preacher. I can look at my own history and present reality and see how he left a legacy of strategy, management, and ministry. Legacy is about faith, hope, love, and joy. It is about passing on that core belief that we can make a difference. I will know I have left a legacy when I see my sons believe that they can make a difference in someone else's life. Legacy has nothing to do with money. Our inheritance to our families, our legacy, is the way we live and demonstrate our values and core beliefs, thus passing them on to the next generation.

ACTIVATION QUESTIONS

1. We will leave a legacy as a father if we understand the significance of our role as a father. How aware are you of your significance in the lives of your children?

2. What legacy would you like to leave your children?

30. FATHERS RESTORE LOST YEARS

In Joel 2:25, God promises that He will restore the years the locusts have eaten. I lost my dad when I was fifteen years old, but I still remember sitting with him on the front row in Lord's Pavilion to watch cricket, or going to concerts with him. A couple of years before he died, he was given a ticket to a soccer match. While I would have loved to go, and he would have loved to take me, there was only the one ticket. I knew it broke his heart to not share the experience because he always tried to do things together.

Taking my son to the World Cup to watch England play live in Brazil was a form of restoration for that previously lost experience with my own father. It was something my son always wanted to do, and something I wanted to share with him.

Fathers have an invitation to live with the intention of giving away what they may never have received themselves. If we fail to learn how to walk in sonship on our way to becoming fathers, we are at risk of acting out of self-pity rather than restoration or redemption. If I'm constantly saying, "Poor me, look at what I didn't have," I'll miss out on redeeming those lost years. I'll tell my kids, "I didn't have it, so why should you?" The opportunity we have as fathers is to understand what we never had or received, and become that, or give that, to our own children. We get to serve our families by filling the gap and fighting so that our sons don't have to.

The word "redeem" means to repair or restore the value of something, to "offset the bad effect of," or "to make worthwhile" (Merriam-Webster). We often think that where we have lack, we also lack value. Through redemption, God restores value where we previously didn't perceive anything of worth. Where there is a loss, a father has the opportunity to turn the loss into gain. While this isn't always practical in the natural, we have an opportunity to co-labor with God to redeem lost years in our own lives and in the lives of our children.

ACTIVATION QUESTIONS

1. As you look over your life do you see any areas in which lost years need restoring or redeeming? Take a few minutes to ask God about them.

2. What would it look like for you to help restore or redeem lost years in your family members' lives?

31. FATHERS CREATE "NORMAL"

Often people equate the word "normal" with things that are bland, uninteresting, or unoriginal. In today's society, we celebrate what is different, unique, and extraordinary—we seek what entertains and thrills us. I love that about the world we live in, and at the same time I believe that everything that is unique and extraordinary comes from a foundation of normal. "That's so vanilla," is a phrase sometimes used to describe something ordinary. Personally, I really like vanilla, particularly vanilla ice cream; it is by no means boring or bland. Nearly all ice cream recipes start with vanilla as the base—it is a vital part of making other great ice cream flavors. And so it is with life. "Normal" is the base required for all of the beautiful and wild "flavors" of life. It is the foundation on which we build.

While vanilla ice cream is just one example of normal, we particularly value the meaning of that word as it pertains to our health. At one point or another, we all have the undesirable experience of having tests done by a doctor, from blood work and MRIs, to CT scans, and mouth swabs. If there is one thing we have in common, it is the desire to have the tests come back normal. In other words, normal equals healthy.

Fathers play a huge role in creating normal, the healthy and basic foundation on which all other recipes—or aspects of life—can be built. In *The Philosophy of Aristotle*, the author and philosopher Aristotle wrote, "Give me a child until he is seven and I will give you the man." His claim was simple: what a child encounters in their formative years will become their normal for the rest of their lives. Creating that normal is vital. The absence of that foundation can cause someone to search all of his life for what is missing. Without a reference point of normal—an inner compass—we'll struggle to determine our direction or purpose.

Fathers, mothers, and grandparents are all vital to the definition of normal in our lives. Jesus is the greatest example of how and why this is the case. He came to a world of sacrifice, laws, and compliance, and revealed a new normal of hope and love. He wasn't introducing an event, but a lifestyle, and we do the same. As parents and grandparents, we create a normal lifestyle and a foundation that our children can return to. Again, we can look at the example of the son in Luke 15. Is it possible that part of what helped him come to his right mind was the realization of how far he had strayed from the family's normal? Perhaps it was this thought that prompted a need to go back home and re-establish the normal that he had lost. Without that foundation, however, there is no internal compass to guide us.

It is important to note that normal varies from country to country and from family to family. I spent fifteen years living in the United States, and there were times when I was very aware of the differences between life there and life in the United Kingdom, and other times when those differences went unnoticed. Since being back in the UK the most obvious challenge has been driving. In fifteen years of living in the USA I established a normal that isn't normal in my current country. I can no longer turn right on a red light and I have to relearn which direction to look first when I come to a cross street.

Our experiences of normal will differ depending on the careers we choose, the way we were raised, and the daily habits we formed as children, but creating some type of normal is still important. I was raised in an era when shops remained closed on Sundays and it was considered a day of rest, different from every other day of the week. Now that times have changed and shopping on Sunday is a new normal, Sunday instinctively still feels like a special day to me. Disciplines were established in my life when I was young that continue to guide me today.

These disciplines, our understanding of a foundational norm, are not just established when we are children. Sometimes we learn new normals throughout our life. While it is a father's role to help establish normal, sometimes fathers fulfill that role later in life or with those who aren't their children, but their larger church family. In reality, this is what discipleship is—helping people, when they become Christians, to establish a new normal in their lives so that they experience more than just a single moment of salvation, but are introduced to a new way of life. In salvation and discipleship, we establish a new foundation to be guided by throughout our lives. The normal we carry is powerful.

My two sons are very different from one another in many respects. They chose different careers, they have different strengths, and they see life through unique lenses. However, they also have many similarities, behaviors, and practices that were established out of growing up in the same understanding of normal. While some of that understanding came directly through instruction and guidance, a lot of what they see as normal comes from what they experienced in everyday family life. Whether we are aware of doing so or not, fathers are vital to creating that normal, the healthy foundation, the base flavor from which life's recipes are developed.

ACTIVATION QUESTIONS

1. In which areas of life do you feel that you have a well-established normal? Where did that normal come from?

2. Are there any "normal" foundations you have come to base your life on that wouldn't be God's normal for you? What does He want to tell you about these areas?

32. FATHERS ESTABLISH MORAL TRUTH

Fathers establish moral truth for their children and create an environment at home in which truth can be discussed. The Greeks had a trilogy of truth, goodness, and beauty that was said to be the foundation of society. Solzhenitsyn compared this trilogy to three trees in his Nobel Prize winning speech, saying, "If the too obvious, so straight branches of Truth and Good are crushed or amputated and cannot reach the light—yet perhaps the whimsical, unpredictable, unexpected branches of Beauty will make their way through and soar up to that very place and in this way perform the work of all three." That is its own huge subject, but the point is this: Truth is the rational conscience and goodness is the moral conscience. They have been cut down in our age.

Moral truth is the interpretation of the right and wrong way I should live my life according to my beliefs. It covers the rights and wrongs of things like relationships and how I treat other people. Moral truth has often been questioned, but now, so too has rational truth. People claiming that the Holocaust never happened, for example, are attacking rational (factual) truth. This generation is the first to encounter that on a global scale. With the internet, Google, and every other search engine available to us, we can easily find so many opinions and unsubstantiated "facts" to cause you to question both rational and moral truth.

Fathers make space in the home for healthy discussions around these concepts of truth. If there is not healthy debate in the home, children will struggle to find a moral compass or establish it when they leave the home. Out of healthy debate at home comes the ability for things to be talked through without being offensive. It leads to the formation of personal opinions of what is right and wrong from a moral point of view. By engaging our children in that way, fathers create the moral compass: the plumb lines of truth. Teaching sons and daughters truth, and modeling that truth, while allowing for the discovery and pursuit of their own beliefs, is a delicate balance, but fathers are vital in this process.

ACTIVATION QUESTIONS

1. Was there healthy debate in your home as a child, or did you grow up with an aversion to tension and conflict? What does God want to tell you about this?

2. How can you establish moral truth in your own family and sphere?

33. FATHERS CREATE CULTURE

Fathers create the culture and environment of the home. Jesus taught us this in the Beatitudes. Culture is traditions, values, beliefs, practices, and customs that become lived-out behavior, and by which a people group cope with their world. The story language of families—the way that families get together and remember the things they did, the way they celebrated, the things they loved to do and traditions around holidays—those things are all wrapped up in culture.

Remember that fathers "do things" and a father creates culture when he has values and lives them out. In that way, culture can also be defined as "the way we do things around here." Culture can be seen in at least four ways, and the culture created by a father will demonstrate each of these:

1. Culture creates an environment in which to grow. Growth is a natural response to a healthy culture.

2. Culture provides protection. The culture of the home is a safe place.

3. Culture gives a lens to life and how to view it. This comes back partly to moral truth. There are many views and perspectives to be found in the world. Through creating culture, fathers lay down a normal of core beliefs and values that set up a framework for how to view life.

4. Culture affects the way everything else is done.

In today's society, culture often comes from what children see on the internet, television, computer games, movies, and what they learn from friends at school. The truth is that the strongest, most powerful culture that is going to influence our next generation is grown and birthed in the home. Often fathers don't realize that they have the ability to determine culture in this way. My dad was always a good giver of gifts. My memory of my birthday was that there was always something that he'd gone to slightly unusual lengths to buy for me. That is now something I do for my children. I go to great lengths to give slightly unusual gifts when I can. The culture my dad created has become my culture.

ACTIVATION QUESTIONS

1. What influences are crafting the culture that you are living in?

2. How are you intentionally crafting the culture in your home? How do your words and actions lay down core values and beliefs?

34. FATHERS MODEL AFFECTION AND HEALTHY EMOTION

There is no question in my mind that to have affection modeled in the home is vital. Humorous though it may sound, it was thirty-five years at least between the last kiss I experienced from my father and receiving any other type of male affection. There was very little experience of male-to-male affection in my life. Male-to-male affection in today's world has either been made into something abhorrent or made into a joke, yet it is an essential part of our lives and of learning how to relate to God. It has to be modeled in the home, and if it is not, then it will be modeled by the world outside of the home in many other ways that aren't necessarily helpful or healthy. When fathers model affection and healthy emotion, they are defining a normal for their sons and daughters, and creating a reference point that will stand for the rest of their life in contrast to those models displayed by popular culture.

Healthy emotions displayed by men may be one of the greatest deficits of our modern world. For too long it has been taboo for men to express the softer, more tender emotions, especially tears. I am so pleased to see that over the past twenty years there has been a shift to a more permissive culture in this area. The previous expectation that men, and even boys, would withhold their emotion led to many of them not knowing how to process emotions in a healthy way. In many cases this expectation even prevented men from knowing how to acknowledge those emotions. As fathers choose to be authentic and vulnerable, they define a normal in their children that gives permission for them, too, to be authentic and learn how to manage the full range of emotions in a healthy way.

The Bible tells us that we should, "Rejoice with those who rejoice, and weep with those who weep"(Romans 12:15). As well as modeling affection, fathers model how to cope with both the good things and the negative things that happen in life. Fathers teach us how to cope with joy and grief while still being responsible for how we act; and they do so by demonstrating what it looks like to work through conflicting emotions. As Joel Osteen says, "If you're looking to buy a house and the house falls through, there will always be a better one." Fathers walk these divine tensions, and as they do, they teach their kids how to live their lives in the reality of the verse, "He works all things together for the good of those who love Him and are called according to His purpose"(Romans 8:28). In other words, He wastes nothing and He gets you ready. I've modeled that, I believe, to both of my sons, and they live their lives through that lens.

ACTIVATION QUESTIONS

1. How easy do you find it to express healthy emotion and affection?

2. Children may get their view of appropriate emotion and affection from the television, teaching at school, teachers and sports coaches, peers, or popular culture. Where are your children getting their influence from in this area, and how can you influence them in a healthy way?

35. FATHERS CULTIVATE WONDER AND JOY

In his book *Beauty Will Save The World*, Brian Zahnd writes that wonder is mystery and beauty. I will forever love that definition. I think that to be childlike is to forever experience beauty and mystery. When a father demonstrates and expresses what is beautiful to him, and therefore what brings joy to him, he models an appreciation and a value for beauty and for mystery. That is setting a child up for a life of wonder that they never have to grow out of. I love what Tony Campolo says about how God created daisies:

How did God create daisies? I say: [With] the excitement of a little child. That is how God created daisies. He created one daisy… and in the childlike heart of God, He clapped and said, "Do it again!" And He created daisy number two and something within God said, "Do it again!" And He created daisy number three and four and five and fifty billion trillion daisies later, the great God of the universe is still creating with childlike excitement and joy and yelling, "Do it again!"

As we look at this description we see beauty and wonder and mystery all thrown into one. If wonder is beauty and mystery, then to be childlike is to love beauty and mystery. To lie on our backs with our children and gaze at the vastness of the skies together will encourage a life of wonder and embracing mystery. Likewise, pointing to beauty and teaching our children what is beautiful to them will be vital as they grow up and pursue the desires of their hearts put there by our Father in heaven.

One of the lessons I learned in my journey of sonship is the importance of having someone demonstrate how to combat worry by celebrating and having fun in the middle of lack. Personally, I had never had a dad walk into a tough situation in my home and say, "Hey, don't worry about the money, let's just go out for a meal." That external influence—someone stepping in to do what we cannot—demonstrates that "the joy of the Lord is your strength" (Nehemiah 8:10). A father brings joy into a situation where his children are struggling to experience joy. Fathers don't lower everything to the lowest common denominator of a crisis; they model the ability to be mentally healthy despite competing emotions. Fathers bring their joy to their child's place of mourning. It's not light or frivolous, but it is important.

ACTIVATION QUESTIONS

1. In this chapter we learn that to be childlike is to forever experience beauty and mystery. To what degree is childlikeness a reality in your own life?

2. What steps can you take to make room for wonder and joy?

36. FATHERS SHOW THEIR CHILDREN HOW TO LOVE THEIR SPOUSES

In my early days as a pastor I remember having a newly married man in my office. He was experiencing great challenges in those early days of marriage. He had some strong convictions in one area of life, convictions that his wife did not share, and yet they affected his approach to life, marriage, and ministry. My advice to him was simple: as a husband, you need to die to yourself. Fathers and husbands model how to love their wives as Christ loved the church, and of course, He died for her. I remember when my youngest son was doing something for his wife and I commented that he was being courageous. I still have the text exchange on my phone because it was so beautiful. His reply to me was that what he was doing was in him because he had first seen me do it for my wife.

I remember shopping with my dad as a child. He taught me how to buy gifts for my wife by modeling it in his relationship with my mum. I know many men find it difficult to go into a shop to buy lingerie for their wives, but my dad took me into lingerie shops in the high street where we lived to buy gifts for my mum. It might seem like a weird example, but this is how you model affection for your wife. In the absence of a father, the culture that influences somebody in their relationships will come from elsewhere. The way we treat our spouses and demonstrate our love to them doesn't just influence our children and our home, but displays to the children of the world how Christ loves His bride. Paul wrote, "Husbands, love your wives, just as Christ also loved the church and gave Himself up for her" (Ephesians 5:25). Fathers have the great privilege of demonstrating to their children and the world what the love of Christ looks like in a very practical and tangible way.

ACTIVATION QUESTIONS

1. How visible is your love for your spouse to your children and those you do life with?

2. What can you do to make it more visible to them?

THE CONTINUED JOURNEY OF FATHERHOOD

SECTION THREE

37. MAN-TO-MAN

I was recently at a conference in Germany sharing my journey of sonship—the imaginary conversation I had with my Dad, and how it helped me to deal with areas of lack I had from losing him at such a young age. After I taught, I was walking around the city when I began to see a fresh layer of that journey. I can remember a lot of different moments from my childhood: wrestling with Dad in the living room while we watched pro wrestling on the television every Saturday afternoon, playing cricket with him in the park. I have those memories and an understanding of what I lost when he died. As I walked around that beautiful city, I realized afresh that it wasn't just childhood experiences that I lost, but the experience of knowing my father as an adult. I missed out on that unique man-to-man relationship.

Two days later at the same conference, Steve Witt, a good friend of mine, was preaching on the man Jesus—the Jesus we don't ever discuss. Between the age of twelve, when Jesus was at the temple, and the age of thirty, when He was baptized, we know very little about His life. Steve shared about Jesus the carpenter from the little town of Nazareth. It was a small community—maybe He knew Peter or was even involved in working on his boat. Maybe He made yokes for oxen and dolls for children. He probably ate olives and flatbreads and the types of locusts that were kosher, instead of the shrimp that were not. His family would have sat around for hours in the evenings talking.

Steve's brilliant perspective got me thinking. I love inner healing and I get that we want to help people heal their relationship with God. I love watching father wounds melt away as people come to understand His love. But I realize there is more for us than that. We aren't meant to only relate to God as children, but as adults. I want to give and to receive from Jesus, man-to-man, to know more than the cursory back-slaps of a peer, and to walk with Jesus—and other men—in brotherly relationship.

The only country album I own has a song titled, "Beer with Jesus." When I heard that song a few years ago, it touched me because it speaks about sitting late into the evening and having an honest man-to-man conversation with Jesus. That is the type of relationship I want to have with Him, and it is also the type of father I want to be to the adult sons and daughters in my life.

I am often asked for parenting advice and I gladly share about the ups and downs in the journey Sue and I traveled in raising our sons. In my training as a psychiatric nurse, I also gained much knowledge about transactional analysis and parent-child roles. It was all useful information that helped us to parent our children. Now, as a father to adult sons, who I am as a parent has changed, and I realize that we as parents need advice not just in raising our children, but in relating to our adult children.

In our current season, I drive one of my sons twenty minutes to and from the train station each day. Because he is commuting, he has been reading a lot, and I often find myself reading the books and listening to the podcasts he recommends. Out of that has come conversation and discussion that has built connection. He and I are in the midst of building a different kind of relationship than the one we previously had.

When our children become adults, the things we do as fathers are based on a man-to-man relationship rather than the parent-child relationship we have when our children are younger. As their father, we still have a desire to protect, counsel, and guide them. However, it is they who have changed. Our children become adults and we must learn to relate to them as adults.

I want that kind of relationship with the leaders and people around me, but also with Jesus. I want to move beyond relating to Jesus purely as a child, and I want to give and receive from Jesus as an adult as well. It is part of maturing and growing up, relating to our parents as adults and as peers. Learning to walk with Jesus man-to-man is another piece of redemption for me in the loss of my dad. In fact, learning to relate to Jesus as an adult is redeeming for all of us and all of our relationships.

What would it have really been like to walk the streets and the shores of Galilee with Jesus, the man? What would we have seen and learned by watching Him relate to His mother and father and His carpentry customers? As we learn to walk with the man, Jesus, we receive a strength of connection, a backing, and an encouragement that we don't understand when we approach Him only as a child.

Fathers raise sons that become real men. Sometimes our deficits—the relationships we lacked—can keep us trapped in relating to Jesus and those around us purely as children. While childlikeness is beautiful and good, part of our journey in both fatherhood and sonship is learning to grow and mature into people who know how to walk out a man-to-man relationship with Jesus and those around us.

ACTIVATION QUESTIONS

1. What is your relationship with Jesus like? How do you usually relate to Him?

2. Ask Jesus what it might look like to relate to Him differently. What does He have for you in the coming season? How does He want to reveal Himself to you?

38. FATHERING ORGANIZATIONS

You cannot lead an organization without influencing those in the organization and those who are served by it. As soon as any sort of structure is created within the organization, the influence will be felt through that structure. From a nation to a small, local business, there is a common thread of ways in which this influence affects the organization and its stakeholders.

Leading an organization is, I would suggest, akin to fathering it. In other words, the manner in which the leader and the organization function will affect everyone within that organization in the same way the father influences the family. The options available to leaders are also similar to those available to fathers: they will fulfill their role effectively or poorly. Regardless of how they choose to operate, their position as father of their organization will remain. Position has this effect. Staff and customers will recognize the leader as the key influencer. A leader, CEO, or prime minister is looked up to. They become a sort of role model either for how to lead or how not to lead. They can quickly become the one to blame and their impact can be unavoidable if the option to leave the organization is not present.

The title of "father" may not be given to leaders of organizations, but the far-reaching effect of fatherhood will still exist. This will not happen overnight and it may not be immediately obvious, but it will be there.

One of the cultures that is most important in the role of governing an organization is honor. I like to reference three examples of what it looks like to lead by honor. These examples are vital to gathering and fathering an organization and they are the crucial elements of becoming sons who become fathers.

Firstly, we grow from glory to glory through honor. We see this in 2 Corinthians 3:18, "But we all, with unveiled face, beholding as in a mirror the glory of the Lord, are being transformed into the same image from glory to glory, just as from the Lord, the Spirit." When we learn to recognize the glory in others, we are honoring them. That is how we grow to a greater glory or expression of God on earth. We also know that before honor comes humility (Proverbs 15:33). The picture is clear when we transfer this to the organization: when we are willing to create a learning environment, secure in the knowledge of sonship, we have the keys to growth. Growth is not based on looking to ourselves or controlling what happens, but on rightly positioning ourselves.

We read in Isaiah 9:6-7 that government is on the shoulders of a son and the result is increase. How we father an organization will either bring increase or not. It is not always about productivity or success, but about honoring the lives of those we serve or who are served by our organization.

Secondly, we see that the church will be built on honor. When Jesus told Peter that He would build His church on the rock, I believe He was referring to Peter's recognition of who he said Jesus was. The importance of this is, again, honor. It is the ability to recognize Christ as the foundation of the Church. In other words, honor, in this case, is recognizing the glory that Jesus carries as the son of God.

Finally, Matthew 25 explains that nations will be judged by their ability to serve the poor, naked, hungry, sick, and prisoners. Once again, we see a picture of honor. "Then He will answer them, 'Truly I say to you, to the extent that you did not do it to one of the least of these, you did not do it to Me'" (Matthew 25:45).

These three illustrations demonstrate to me that when we are leading people, honor is vital. Without it, there will be pride and dishonor at the roots of both our fathering/leading and the organization or family that we lead. We will reproduce people, behaviors, and cultures based on our function or dysfunction.

Fathers live to bless others, to model the Heavenly Father, and to reproduce those that will do the same. All of the things fathers do in this book will in some way or another apply to the leader of any organization.

When I teach leaders I often suggest creating an overarching job description for them, one which would serve any leader from president to small business owner. Firstly, the leader needs a relationship with God. It is from this relationship, and this relationship alone, that they will be able to lead as a son and reveal the Father. Secondly, they will express the vision of the organization. Leaders may choose to go through the process of vision-casting as a team, but regardless of how they establish the vision, the leader will need to carry it as his or her own. Thirdly, the leader must recognize himself or herself as the face or father of the organization. What this actually looks like depends on the nature, size, and influence of the organization. When it comes to nations, we literally see the faces of leaders on coins and banknotes. The final aspect of the leader's job description is the need to build relationship with other fathers and mothers, inviting them to add strength to the organization.

This job description, and the three illustrations of honor, are all aspects that amount to fathering an organization. Leaders will, of course, also use their own skills and gifts to serve the organization overall. Regardless of what each individual leader carries, their ability to express honor and their role as fathers will determine the culture of their organization and the types of "sons" they produce.

ACTIVATION QUESTIONS

1. Who are you serving, and who is being served by your organization? How do they see you?

2. Are you leading by honor? How can you grow this culture within your organization?

39. THE HEART OF THE MATTER

The Old Testament closes with Malachi 4:6, "He will restore the hearts of the fathers to their children and the hearts of the children to their fathers, so that I will not come and smite the land with a curse." This is the transition verse to the New Testament. The revelation that follows is also about restoration of relationships: Jesus is sent by the Father to reveal the Father, to be about the Father's business, and to lead many sons to glory.

It is hard to miss, therefore, that the knowledge of the Father is not only central to our faith and lives, but is also the essential source of life. As we experience the Father's heart, we are, through Jesus, empowered to reveal the Father to a world that was always predestined to revolve, exist, and thrive on the presence of a Father. This turning of our hearts towards the Father is the answer the world needs to the curse of fatherlessness found in Malachi.

If we get our heart and our view of our Heavenly Father right, everything else in our lives will start to line up. In fact, I would suggest that there is no situation, circumstance, conflict, or lack, which cannot be solved by the restoration of hearts to the Father.

As we consider the heart, we see Jeremiah 17:9, "The heart is deceitful above all things." This is discouraging on its own, but thankfully we find the answer to that dilemma in Hebrews 3:13: "But encourage one another daily, as long as it is called today, so that none of you may be hardened by sin's deceitfulness." Although it is our life-source, these verses are not talking about the physical heart. They are referencing the spiritual heart, the core of our being, the point of contact with others and with our Heavenly Father.

It is not just in the physical body that the heart is the very center of our being, keeping us physically alive. The use of the word "heart" indicates the very center of our being—our soul. It conveys what we love and what we believe. Ensuring that our heart is not deceived is the key to our spiritual life. The physical heart keeps us alive by pumping blood, but the spiritual heart also needs a flow of encouragement and connection to the Father so that it is not hardened.

When someone has a moral fall or has failed in some way, people sometimes ease their discomfort by stating that the fallen person "had a good heart." I know what they are trying to say, and it does make some sense, but it is also incorrect. If the heart is good, physically, then the health of the body is also. The same principle applies to the soul of man. What is often trying to be conveyed is that they tried their best, they had good motives or intentions, but the reality is that the dysfunction in the heart could not be kept hidden forever, and eventually it was exposed. So many of life's failures stem from a "heart" condition.

We can all try our best, but if the heart is not functioning in a healthy way, then sooner or later the weakness will be exposed, and the recovery and restoration process will need to involve an examination of the heart. Teaching on the Father's heart and sonship is, in my view, inseparable from what many call inner healing. I would suggest that the vast majority of inner healing sessions relate to dysfunctional experiences in relationships on earth, and that they therefore affect our relationships with Father, Son, and Holy Spirit.

Let's be a generation that gets the heart right. I love the culture created by many friends of ours where they ask each other how their heart is. We need that, according to Hebrews 3:13, in order to prevent the devastating truth of Jeremiah's description of the heart's deceitfulness.

We have seen throughout this book that the state of the heart influences behavior—individually, in families, organizations, nations, and our global society. When the influence of fathers is removed, society is changed. I believe it is suffering from the curse which is contained in Malachi 4:6. I do not see this as an act of punishment by God, but the consequence of the removal of fathers and their influence from our world.

Kris Vallotton recently preached and wrote a blog about the effects of fatherlessness. He identifies that the effects of removing the influence of fathers from our world touch every aspect of our lives. We lack leaders in homes, families, and nations, and we see jails filled, suicide rates rising, and increasing numbers of dropouts from schools, colleges, and universities. These statistics, as well as the number of children running away from home, and an increase in sexual crimes, all have a direct correlation to fatherlessness. You can find Kris' teaching on his website krisvallotton.com.

Mordecai is a hero in the Bible and an example of what it looks like to father those who are not our natural children, those who need fathers. In adopting Esther, he adopted an orphan who would one day have great influence. Perhaps we can look at Mordecai as a prototype of what we are all to become. The ones who adopt the orphaned influencer, preparing the way for us to understand more fully the meaning of Malachi 4:6.

The foundation of the things fathers do must be re-established. Without it, the curse of fatherlessness will continue to create a world without moral compass, lacking identity, searching for home, for normal, and for identity. Without fathers being fathers, we lack the example of how to love our wives, how to be part of a family from which we grow, mature, and are sent out to reveal the Father in the things we do and say.

Our world is challenged by an unhealthy view of identity, relationships, value for life, truth and goodness, and distorted views of beauty, to name a few. The answer, the heart of the matter, is that we turn our hearts back to the Father, and restore the relationship of the children to their fathers. As we turn to God and allow Him to heal our hearts, we will become the fathers we were always meant to be. We will do things.

ACTIVATION QUESTIONS

1. Can you see the influence of the Father on your own heart? How does His touch manifest itself in your life?

2. Does your heart need healing? Take the opportunity to spend some time with your Heavenly Father, asking Him about how your heart is looking. Is it time to get help from a friend or pastor, or schedule an inner healing session?

40. THE FATHER'S TOOLKIT

As I came to the end of writing this book, I began to think of things that get handed down through the generations. I am sure that many of you own a toolkit, perhaps even with some tools that have been handed down from your father. Maybe the "tools" that have been handed down to you include china, furniture, or other family heirlooms. Sometimes we inherit things when we are too young to understand the value of what we have received. However, somewhere along the way, life happens and things become more complex. Suddenly the value of simple things is realized.

I began to think that perhaps there is a "Father's toolkit," not cameras, tools, or kitchen knives, but attitudes, behaviors, and responses that we carry inside of ourselves, ready to reveal the Father at a moment's notice. Taking my lead from Luke 15, I began to build one. I would like to close by encouraging you to build one, too. These are the basic tools, the hammers and screwdrivers, the knives and spoons of the father's toolkit. Let us rebuild the tools that fathers always carry with them, tools that will be passed on to the generations after us.

The father in Luke 15 was waiting for his son to return. He did not know his son would be returning that day, but he carried with him an attitude of expectation. As soon as he saw his son, he ran, and as soon as he met him, he responded. I want to be ready to reveal the Father in the same way that father was ready to receive his son home. I have used the elements of the father's gifts to his son in Luke 15 to convey the different tools in our kit. "But the father said to his slaves, 'Quickly bring out the best robe and put it on him, and put a ring on his hand and sandals on his feet; and bring the fattened calf, kill it, and let us eat and celebrate'" (Luke 15: 22-23). I pray that this toolkit makes us all ready.

Trust

The Ring. This small item was a symbol of trust. The ring is the modern-day equivalent of the credit card for the family business. A signet ring in those days would often be used to seal letters and contracts. The boy's speech contained the request to be treated as a servant. He was not asking to be trusted or restored to his original status. No doubt his experiences of failure had made it difficult for him to trust himself. He was likely looking for rules to be imposed as he had lost the ability to trust his inner regulators. But a key to trusting ourselves is being trusted by others. We all need a ring in our pockets, so to speak, ready for those who have lost trust in themselves. A ring to help others start the journey of trusting again. Becoming a believable or trustworthy person begins with self-trust, but when we don't have that, the trust of a father will more than likely kick-start the journey towards self-trust. How do we trust someone who has let us down or doesn't feel trustworthy? There comes a point when we must learn to trust again. Fathers do that: they restore trust.

Value

The Robe. How many around us feel unworthy? People exist covered in shame instead of self-worth. The robe was the symbol conveying value and worth. There is no reference in the story of the boy having a shower before he was welcomed home. He wasn't required to scrub himself clean. The outside appearance was not the issue. The extravagant symbol of worth cleared the way for the internal man to feel clean and worthy again. Whether we find ourselves needing to express value and worth to our own son or daughter, or someone else's, there comes a point where valuing the outward person allows the inside to begin feeling worthy again. This external treatment will change the person's own view of themselves. The son was likely feeling worthless. Perhaps on the journey home he had visualized taking a bath before meeting his dad. Those plans were irrelevant because the father got there first. No matter how hard we try to scrub ourselves clean, the Father cleanses the inner man. By placing the robe reserved for special guests on his son, the father in Luke 15 made a very loud and clear statement: You are worthy. While we were yet sinners the Bible says that Christ died for us (Romans 5:8). While we smelled of pigs, He placed a robe of righteousness on us. Can we learn to do this, to express worth before we try and clean someone up?

Identity

The Sandal. This is the Jewish symbol of sonship. We are surrounded by people who do not know their identity. They do not understand that they are not alone, that there is a Father who gives us our identity. The son in our story had prepared his speech, declaring that he was no longer a son. Yet, the father restored his identity as son. That is our role as fathers; restoring identity. John the Baptist could not reinforce Jesus's identity by tying his sandals. He was His cousin, he knew who he was, yet he knew that he was not worthy to do this. It was a father's job to declare and confirm identity. Just after John's statement, Jesus is baptized, the whole heavenly family is there and in that environment, God the Father says, "This is my beloved Son" (Matthew 3:17). The Father put the "sandal" on the feet of Jesus. Are we ready, as natural and spiritual fathers, with our sandal and symbol of sonship? Are we ready with the words necessary to call forth and confirm the identity of our sons and daughters? Even Saul in 1 Samuel 17:55 did this, confirming David as a son with influence and significance. He looked at David and asked, "Whose son is that?" Fathers call forth identity. Are we ready?

Presence

The father waiting for his son to return. Isn't this a beautiful thought; being missed, longed-for, and seen, even when we do not feel seen? In Luke 15:31, the father is speaking to the elder son, "And he said to him, 'Son, you have always been with me, and all that is mine is yours.'" The father was with him all along, and yet the elder brother did not experience the father's presence. It is the same for us. The Father is with us and we have an opportunity to be aware of His presence in our lives.

Conversely, it is possible for us to feel alone even when we are surrounded by those who love us. Moses understood this well. He had seen so much, but he arrived at a place in his journey where he told God that if He did not go with them, it was not worth going. We all have a need and a desire to feel sent and supported so that in our hearts we are able to access the love of our fathers and mothers.

Fathers provide presence. This accessibility and availability is a powerful gift. Sometimes our sons and daughters just need to be reminded that we are there for them. Like the elder son, our kids need to be reminded that all we have is available to them and we are present in their lives.

Provision

The father's words in Luke 15 to the elder brother can be easily overlooked and yet they convey a need which we all have. Revealing God the Provider to our children may not always include being able to provide everything for our children, but rather creating a culture of provision. The elder brother felt ignored. He had worked hard for no reward and watched with jealousy as the younger brother, who had done nothing, received so much. Once again the real issue is what is happening on the inside, in his heart. The elder brother had enjoyed all of the benefits of being at home, but he had not accessed the privilege of provision within his heart. Sometimes we need to be woken up to gratitude. This can happen when we watch someone being given what they don't deserve, or when we see someone who has very little express appreciation for what little they have. Familiarity rightly breeds contempt and we all need to be reminded of what we have available to us.

As fathers, we get the enormous privilege of this action. We step in and give what is not deserved. It is such a powerful example of revealing the Father who gave us, through His son, what none of us deserved and could never work for. Not only that, but He continues to declare that He will always be with us: presence and provision.

Celebration

When the father told the servants to kill the fatted calf, we are privy to a moment of complete extravagance. He demonstrated to the crowd, especially the religious zealots, the celebration of sinners who repent and return home. It is vital that the ability to celebrate is in our toolbox. When I was in charge of a young offender prison, I regularly held graduation services for a particular educational course. It was something I greatly enjoyed and also a special moment for the families, as well. It gave them an opportunity to celebrate their sons and grandsons who, by the time they entered prison, had likely failed and caused disappointment many times over. The boys and the families needed a reason to celebrate.

We all have a need to be celebrated, especially when we lose trust in ourselves, feel unworthy, and lose sight of our true identity. In those moments, celebration has the capacity to restore the course of our lives.

From the simple day-to-day, to the moments of breakthrough, victory, or accomplishment, these tools are a powerful resource. All of us want and need to be valued, known, trusted, seen, provided for, and celebrated. And what a privilege it is that you and I, as fathers, get to reveal these aspects of the Father's heart to our children.

ACTIVATION QUESTIONS

1. Which tool in this toolkit are you most in need of at the moment? Ask the Father about that area.

2. Take a few minutes to build your own father's toolkit. What do you find in yours? How can you use each tool to bring life to those you father?

41. YOU LIVE THE FINAL CHAPTER

It is absolutely extraordinary that Jesus will be known for all eternity as a son—though He had no earthly father—and as a father—though He had no earthly sons. Not only does He carry His identity as a Son and Father into heaven, but by adopting us as sons and daughters, He brings us into heaven's relational family as princes and princesses.

We see this continual journey of sonship here on earth in the story of Job. At the beginning of the book, Job loses everything, but at the end we find Job, at 140 years of age, with four generations of sons alive. That means there are sons who are over a hundred years old, grandsons in their eighties, and great-grandsons in their fifties. It is easy to restrict our view of generational sonship to young kids, a middle-aged dad, and a grandfather who is an old guy. Sonship and fatherhood go beyond this snapshot in time. We all change and mature into new roles and relationships throughout our lives, passing the baton as we move from being a son, to being the father of young children, to fathering teens and then men. We move from father to grandfather in relationships that grow and morph, fathers honoring the sons, and sons honoring the fathers, passing the baton while we are both still running. Sonship is an eternal journey, and a beautiful one.

As I come to the end of this book, it is worth mentioning that there is no end to the journey of sonship and fatherhood. This is merely a launching pad. My goal is to launch you into the eternal journey of sonship and the continual learning of things fathers do. There is only one identity that matters—our identity as sons. It is from this identity that we learn to carry out the many roles of our lives, and none so important as this crucial role of being fathers. Far from being an orphan planet, this world has a Father. What it needs is its sons and daughters to be connected with that Heavenly Father. Once you step into a multigenerational family of sons, you step into a hope that has been nourished for generations. As fathers do things, they have the capacity and ability to be bringers of the solutions that the world needs. Solutions are brought by mothers and fathers, and grandfathers and grandmothers, as they act as mediators and signposts, modeling who the Father is to the world. As we reveal the Father through the way we live and things we do, we reveal that He is the answer to every single problem on this planet. What an incredible privilege that we get to run this journey.

As you come to the end of this book, I pray that you have encountered God, learned something, or experienced revelation. Maybe you have been validated in some of the things that you already do as a father, or seen some things you need to do more of. Maybe you've broken lies that have prevented you from stepping into your identity as a father. Whatever your experience of this book has been, there is more to come. That is one of the beautiful truths that we see in the Bible. Jesus said that we would do greater works. He signaled that we would not just do more, but also create a culture that always believed that there is more to come.

And that's where I want to end. There is more. There is more on this journey and in this life. Perhaps you are a son who has not yet become a father. Perhaps you are a man who is not yet married. Maybe you are a father with a young son or daughter, or a father with adult sons and daughters. You may be a grandfather or even a great-grandfather. I want to tell you that wherever you are on this journey, there is more. More to grow in, to learn, more breakthroughs to walk in, more lies and doubts and fears to overcome.

There is more opportunity to do things that reveal the Father, not based in the law, but in the privilege of being princes and sons of the most high God, serving the King and serving the people. That is our great privilege in this life. So as you come to the end, don't stop. Maybe you'll reread this book, maybe you'll go back to the questions, or challenge yourself in an area. Maybe you'll take the message and share it with other people. The most important thing is that this is a journey that never ends. I can tell you that the greatest privilege in my life is when people say that they know me not as much by what I say, but as a father. I don't know any greater privilege than that.

There is more. Keep pursuing.

ACTIVATION QUESTIONS

1. What has most impacted you as you have read through *Things Fathers Do*? What will you take away with you?

2. What one change will you make this week in the way that you consider yourself as a father, or treat those around you? How will your world look different in a year, if you enact this change?

ABOUT PAUL

Paul Manwaring is a member of the senior leadership team at Bethel Church in Redding, California. After fifteen years in Redding, he now resides back in the UK with his wife, Sue. He is still surprised at what he gets to do in life—believing in a God who has never let him down, and a life where he knows that God wastes nothing and gets him ready.

Paul speaks and travels widely to equip and encourage the global body of Christ to demonstrate the glory of the Kingdom of God. His main interests lie in what it means to be a father, organizational management, personal development for leaders, and healthcare and healing.

He spent nineteen years in senior prison management in England, is a registered general and psychiatric nurse, and holds a management degree from Cambridge University.

Paul and Sue enjoy being part of the lives of their sons and their spouses and two grandsons, now that they are back home in the UK. When not traveling and teaching, Paul can be found with his family, making and enjoying good food and coffee.

FURTHER RESOURCES

What on Earth is Glory?

Preachers often quote this majestic promise in describing the consummation of history, the restoration of all things at the end of time. But few seek to uncover the passion of God in this promise: He wants us to know His glory, and He wants us to know it here on earth. What on Earth Is Glory? is one man's journey into this desire of God. From Mt. Sinai to the Cross, from a solitary confinement cell to the snowboarding slopes of Mammoth Lakes, from fathers and mothers to sons and daughters, from time to eternity, Paul Manwaring traces the revelation of God's glory, uncovering the patterns of His divine design and purpose in all things, and inviting others to join him in making the audacious request Moses made millennia ago: "Show me Your glory."

Kisses From A Good God

Author Paul Manwaring was diagnosed with prostate cancer in January 2008. Kisses from a Good God recounts his journey from the first diagnosis, through the prayers of believing friends and family, his choice to undergo surgery, and to his ultimate healing victory.

Kisses from a Good God provides encouragement and challenges some commonly held beliefs. He removes shame from those who have been healed by the hands of doctors and surgeons rather than through prayer. Instead of simply encouraging you with practical, biblical truths, a clear line is drawn between faith and religion—and redefines victory through the eyes of a cancer survivor saved by God in the form of modern medicine.

If you are now walking or have walked through a life-threatening illness or circumstance, or if you have watched a loved one endure, Kisses from a Good God relieves your body, soul, mind, and spirit of tons of unnecessary pressures and pain.

Ways to connect with Paul:

 @Paul_Manwaring

 paul_manwaring

 Paul Manwaring

 www.paulmanwaring.com